The Black Arch

GHOST LIGHT

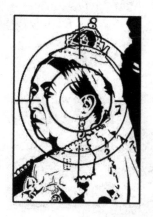

By Jonathan Dennis

Published July 2016 by Obverse Books

Cover Design © Cody Schell

Text © Jonathan Dennis, 2016

Range Editor: Philip Purser-Hallard

2 4 6 8 10 3 5 7 9

Jonathan would like to thank:

Philip and Stuart for the opportunity. Simon Bucher-Jones, Kelly Hale, Dave Hoskin, Greg Harris, Chad Knueppe and Neville McJunkin for the feedback and support. Greg Proops (The Smartest Man in the World) for breadth of knowledge. Sam Seder, Michael Brooks and Matt Binder (The Majority Report) for depth of knowledge. Finally, everyone involved in the production of Ghost Light *for making such a wonderful story to examine.*

To my wife, Wendy.

Also Available

CONTENTS

OVERVIEW

Serial Title: *Ghost Light*

Writer: Marc Platt

Director: Alan Wareing

Original UK Transmission Dates: 4 October 1989 – 18 October 1989

Running Time: Episode 1: 24m 17s

Episode 2: 24m 18s

Episode 3: 24m 17s

UK Viewing Figures: Episode 1: 4.2 million

Episode 2: 4.0 million

Episode 3: 4.0 million

Regular Cast: Sylvester McCoy (The Doctor), Sophie Aldred (Ace)

Guest Cast: Ian Hogg (Josiah), Sylvia Syms (Mrs Pritchard), Michael Cochrane (Redvers Fenn-Cooper), Sharon Duce (Control), Katharine Schlesinger (Gwendoline), John Nettleton (Reverend Ernest Matthews), Carl Forgione (Nimrod), Brenda Kempner (Mrs Grose), Frank Windsor (Inspector Mackenzie), John Hallam (Light)

Antagonists: Josiah Samuel Smith, Light

Novelisation: Doctor Who: *Ghost Light* by Marc Platt. **The Target Doctor Who Library** #149

Responses:

'...a contender for the **Doctor Who** story with the best first episode, and it's interesting, clever and atmospheric.'

[Lance Parkin, 'A Forty-Year Adventure in time and Space', *Time Unincorporated 1: The Doctor Who Fanzine Archives*]

'...in spite of Alan Wareing's direction, it's nothing more than a series of creepy set pieces without any cohesion.'

[Graeme Burk, *Who's 50: 50 Doctor Who Stories To Watch Before You Die – An Unofficial Companion*, p298]

SYNOPSIS

Episode 1

In 1883 the Dean of Mortarhouse College Oxford, the **Rev Ernest Matthews**, visits the home of **Josiah Samuel Smith**, to argue with him about his support for Charles Darwin's 'ungodly' theory of evolution. At nightfall the day-time housekeeper **Mrs Grose** hurries away, leaving him to her nocturnal counterpart, **Mrs Pritchard**.

Matthews is not the first enemy of Josiah's to visit the house: upstairs the explorer and big-game hunter **Redvers Fenn-Cooper** languishes, having lost his sanity when confronted with a mysterious blazing light – a light which still assails him in his cell and which, as **the Doctor** and **Ace** discover after their arrival in the house, may be irradiating him. When Mrs Pritchard returns him to his confinement, the pair meet Josiah's butler, a Neanderthal named **Nimrod**, whose respect the Doctor secures with the gift of a totemic cave-bear tooth. Nimrod takes them to the drawing-room, where Josiah's ward **Gwendoline** is with Matthews. The Dean mistakes the Doctor for Josiah and argues with him until Smith arrives. Ace and Gwendoline experiment with cross-dressing.

At dinner the conversation is interrupted by a wordless phone call from Josiah's 'observatory' in the cellar, where Nimrod has been assaulted. Ace learns from Matthews that Josiah's house is Gabriel Chase, an abandoned 'haunted house' in Perivale where she experienced a trauma as a troubled 13-year-old in 1983. The Doctor has brought her here as an 'initiative test'. Upset, she storms off to the cellar, which contains a stone control room. There she is menaced by shambling animal-headed figures in dinner-suits and taunted by the coarse, malevolent voice of **Control**.

Episode 2

Ace and Nimrod struggle with the bestial figures, mindless former bodies of Josiah's which he has transcended in his personal 'evolution' to become human. During the fight, one of the husks frees Control, while Ace breaks a window-like membrane behind which something else is hibernating. This also puts the stone spaceship in danger of a catastrophic explosion, which the Doctor and Josiah arrive in time to quell. The four are pursued from the cellar by Control, a 'depraved monstrosity' (according to Josiah) which demands its 'freeness'.

Upstairs again, the house's night-time inhabitants retire for the day – Josiah with Matthews, who begins devolving into an ape as Smith begins the next phase of his own evolution. Given the run of the place, the Doctor frees Redvers and **Inspector Mackenzie** of Scotland Yard, who arrived two years ago to investigate the disappearance of Gabriel Chase's former owner, Sir George Pritchard, and has been kept in suspended animation ever since. In a trance state, Nimrod tells the Doctor how his tribe encountered a godlike being of light in his native era.

As evening arrives, Mackenzie identifies Mrs Pritchard and Gwendoline as Sir George's wife and daughter. Sir George has 'gone to Java', which is Gwendoline's euphemism for the murders she now commits at Josiah's behest. Josiah has shed another body and completed his transformation into a Victorian gentleman, while Matthews is now an inert ape-man in a display case. At the Doctor's behest and in return for his promise of freedom, Control emerges from the basement, leading the sleeper from the spaceship, whose name – and appearance – is **Light**.

Episode 3

Light manifests itself as an angel, but is in fact the leader of an extraterrestrial survey party cataloguing Earth's fauna, who added Nimrod to his collection millennia ago. While Light has slept, however, his crew have evolved their own agendas. Control wishes for freedom and to become 'a ladylike', while Josiah has developed a convoluted plan to take over the British Empire. This involves Redvers, who has an invitation to Buckingham Palace, shooting Queen Victoria as a game animal called 'the crowned Saxe-Coburg'.

Light is baffled and threatened by these changes, and affronted by humanity's evolution in particular. Seeking to understand it, he dismembers a maid and reduces Mackenzie to primordial soup, which Mrs Pritchard serves at dinner. She and Gwendoline recover their memories after the Doctor shows them a pendant with their cameo images in it, but Light decrees that they must change no more, and turns them into statues. Increasingly obsessed, he decides to blow up the spaceship in a firestorm which will eradicate all life – and all change – on Earth. The Doctor tells him that all things change including Light himself, and the survey is incomplete. He names missing imaginary and legendary beasts, paralysing him with confusion.

Meanwhile, Nimrod has rejected both his employer and his god, while Control has been taking lessons in 'ladylike' behaviour from Redvers and Ace. Redvers proves that he, too, has cast off Josiah's dominance when he passes his invitation to Control, not Josiah. She burns it and the three of them take Josiah in hand, diverting the spaceship's energy to leave Earth together.

Unable to adapt, Light dissipates – leaving only the lingering sense of evil which the younger Ace will exorcise a century hence, by burning down Gabriel Chase.

1. 'I WANTED TO SEE HOW IT WORKS' I: ANGELS IN THE ARCHITECTURE

Ghost Light (1989) was the end. *Survival* (1989) may have aired afterwards. Books and audio dramas kept different aspects of the series on life-support until it could be brought back[1]. There was the temporary blip of the Paul McGann TV movie, *Doctor Who* (1996), but for a long time this was the last **Doctor Who** story made to be broadcast for a general audience[2]. As the last story of that original 26-year run, it is the story that points the way towards what style of show it would be when it came back. Think about it – it's not that hard to imagine *Ghost Light* done as a modern episode. It's practically the right running time already[3].

Ghost Light is the best argument that the series that ran from 1963 to 1989 is the same one that is currently airing, with only an extended hiatus in between. Certainly, the period of time that passed and the near-complete change in personnel[4] would lead you to think otherwise. Many would point to the changes in style and content, but the question really is, if **Doctor Who** had

---

[1] Though they went about this in different ways. The books focused on what **Doctor Who** would be if it continued, while the audios were more concerned with recreating how it was remembered.

[2] And no, I'm not going to count *Dimensions in Time* (1993) or *Death Comes to Time* (webcast, 2001) or *Scream of the Shalka* (webcast, 2003) or whatever thing you thought of that I didn't just name. And neither should you.

[3] The running time on the back of the DVD release is 71 minutes. Even without allowing for recaps at the beginning of episodes 2 and 3 and the extra credits, it is shorter than *Deep Breath* (2014).

[4] Before you ask, Mike Tucker.

continued uninterrupted, would it be that different from what we have now? The show has a history of changing with the times, incorporating new styles and technologies, such as colour and Colour Separation Overlay. Even accounting for that, *Ghost Light* stood out as an oddity at the time. The thing you hear most often about it is that it was convoluted and difficult to understand. In fact, this is the principal comment you hear repeated during the commentary on the DVD. The qualities that contribute to that perception are the same ones that make the story a forerunner of what was to come.

In an article in the online journal, *i-Perception*, James E Cutting and others researched films from 1935 to 2010 and found four principal changes over time:

> 'First, shot lengths have gotten shorter, a trend also reported by others. Second, contemporary films have more motion and movement than earlier films. Third, in contemporary films shorter shots also have proportionately more motion than longer shots, whereas there is no such relation in older films. And finally films have gotten darker.'[5]

What they researched were Hollywood films, but as we're going to see, **Doctor Who** is a show that is always influenced by what is going on in other media and even a cursory comparison of stories from different years of **Doctor Who** would show that these four changes have happened there as well. Not only that, but when you watch *Ghost Light*, you realise that it is closer to the current end of this spectrum than most 20th-century (what you might think of as

---

[5] Cutting, James E, et al, 'Quicker, faster, darker: Changes in Hollywood film over 75 years'. *i-Perception*, 30 September, 2011.

'classic') **Doctor Who**. As an example, take the first part of that research, shot length. The opening shot of 'An Unearthly Child'[6] from 1963 is a minute and half long. The opening shot of *Rose* (2005) is 11 seconds. The first post-credits shot in *Ghost Light* is three seconds long. (This is something the other stories from that year share. *Survival*'s opening shot is the same length and *The Curse of Fenric*'s is 5 seconds.) It's not just a matter of length either. It's what they're using that time to do. The opening of 'An Unearthly Child' is a long, slow establishing shot and this is something that is simply not done in modern television unless the show is making a point of breaking stylistic norms. The establishing shots of the exterior of Gabriel Chase used throughout *Ghost Light* are seconds long.

I don't think anyone would argue the point that film and television have become faster-paced over the years. The entire career of Michael Bay is predicated on that fact. This faster pace fundamentally changes the way stories are told and how the audience absorbs them. Even so, for the year it was aired, *Ghost Light* is a rapidly paced story. Some of this is due to production issues. In order to make the running time, several scenes were shortened or deleted. Though if you look at the deleted scenes on the DVD, I can't say they would have made it easier to understand – and keep in mind that these scenes made it as far as being shot, so presumably they were deemed more important than ones deleted at the scripting stage.

In drawing and cartooning, there is a concept called 'economy of line': the idea that it is desirable to convey the greatest amount of

---

[6] *An Unearthly Child* episode 1.

information in the fewest pen, pencil or brush strokes. That concept has worked its way into the world of scripting, as filmed media has moved away from being simply filmed theatre and evolved into its own art form. Modern script doctors will tell you to start a scene as late as possible, convey the necessary information of that scene, and end it as soon as possible. Not a second should be wasted. This evolution in thought on how to script has been taking place over decades and *Ghost Light* was ahead of the curve.

What makes *Ghost Light* difficult for some to understand is that it demands close attention. If you try watching it with one eye while doing something else, you will be lost. With video or DVD, the viewer has the option of pausing or rewinding and reviewing what they missed, but it's easy to see how someone watching a live broadcast could be lost. Every scene is important. Every line has meaning; many lines have more than one. In addition, with this level of density in the script, think how difficult it must have been to try and keep track of everything as the three episodes were aired once a week. *Ghost Light* is the first **Doctor Who** story that practically demands binge watching.

These visual and structural changes aren't the only thing that predicts the shape of the series to come. The stories in season 26, especially *Ghost Light* and *Survival*, are about Ace in a way that no previous stories had been about the companion. This wasn't just meeting up with a relative we had never heard of before[7]; it was a focus on the companion's emotional life, her past and her struggles. When the show returned on a regular basis in 2005, the focus was on Rose Tyler and how the events in those stories affect

---

[7] Tegan was especially gifted in this area.

her. For more detail on that aspect of the revival, I'd recommend *The Black Archive #1: Rose* by Jon Arnold[8].

Also note that in *Ghost Light*, Ace's story is not just central for our benefit. Ace's back story is presented to us as being of interest because the Doctor finds it so. His curiosity about her past is the motivation behind his involvement in the story. The Doctor is, if not necessarily the viewpoint character for the audience, the one who draws our attention to what is important. We didn't know much about the inner lives of previous companions because it wasn't a priority in those stories, and the Doctor didn't make it a priority either. The Doctor's fascination with the personal lives of his companions is an element that *Ghost Light* introduced that has stayed with the series to this day. You might say *The Curse of Fenric* (1989) did it first if you wanted to follow intended order rather than air dates, but the Doctor's interest in Ace's background in that story is more related to her lineage, as a pawn in the game with Fenric, rather than her as a person.

Another aspect the story shares with the modern series is its treatment of the Doctor himself. The Doctor started as a mysterious figure who we saw from Ian and Barbara's point of view, and the companions for a long time were the viewpoint character for the audience – but the series kept running. Even though the Doctor's backstory and character were revealed in dribs and drabs, eventually we wound up in a situation where, as companions came and went, the audience knew more about the Doctor than they did. Script Editor Andrew Cartmel tried to re-

---

[8] You are buying all of these, right? You should, or I'm never going to get my chance to explain what went wrong with *Daleks in Manhattan* (2007).

inject some mystery in the character during the Sylvester McCoy years (1987-89) with hints about things in the Doctor's past that the audience didn't know. The 21st-century revival did the same thing with the cataclysmic events of the Time War that were only hinted at, at least initially.

The pacing, the change of focus to the companion, the presaging of 2010-17 showrunner Steven Moffat's love of haunted houses, the addition of a complex subtext[9]: all of these are things that make *Ghost Light* a model for what was to come.

I do want to mention one last thing here. I am going to be talking about *Ghost Light* chiefly in terms of the three episodes as they aired on television and were subsequently presented on home video and DVD. I may mention deleted scenes or material from the novelisation or interviews, but the three episodes represent the final product of all the decisions made by those involved in the production. Any thing else is secondary. Which leads me to the question of 'Lungbarrow'.

In the wilderness days, when fans pondered the true nature of the Cartmel Master Plan[10] and batted theories back and forth on the Usenet boards and mailing lists of old[11], the story Marc Platt originally pitched was treated by some as the great lost **Doctor Who** masterpiece, and *Ghost Light* as just a pale imitation of what might have been. It's easy to see why some elements of fandom

---

[9] Which, let's face it, is not present in a large segment of previous stories.

[10] And it was always capitalised. Trust me. I was there.

[11] 'What are Usenet boards, grandfather?' They were like Facebook but without the inspirational slogans over pictures of flowers, and therefore 1,000 times better.

would find the original idea more attractive. 'Lungbarrow' is focused on the Doctor's background as opposed to Ace's, and thus has that cachet of being the secret origin story that used to have such appeal. I say 'used to' because it's difficult to think of a long-withheld mystery in popular fiction that was finally revealed and not a disappointment. In this respect, John Nathan-Turner was absolutely correct in thinking that 'Lungbarrow' would have revealed too much, too soon. And really, Gallifrey is almost always better in conception than realisation. *The Deadly Assassin* (1976) is the exception. Every time since, when Gallifrey is announced as coming up, the audience hopes it's going to be that good and it never is[12].

Platt and Cartmel made the wise decision to take the essence of 'Lungbarrow' and make it Ace's story rather than the Doctor's. It's a win all around. The Doctor gets to retain his mystery. Ace continues to be more fleshed out as a character than any companion until 2005. A difficult-to-realise alien setting is changed to Victorian England and, as a result, *Ghost Light* looks great as well[13]. Those who absolutely had to have 'Lungbarrow' eventually got the book written by Marc Platt for Virgin's **New Adventures** range[14]. It's substantially different from what would have made it to the screen, of course. It's a 250-page novel instead of a three-part television drama, with all the attendant lack of budgetary concern that entails. It was also written close to a decade later, and was tasked

---

[12] Though *Hell Bent* (2015) makes the wise choice to limit its Gallifrey locations to outside the corridors of the Capitol for as much as possible, and thus succeeds.
[13] Mostly.
[14] Platt, Marc, *Lungbarrow* (1997).

with closing out a continuing novel series and all of its ongoing threads, rather than being one story out of four in a season that no-one at the time knew was the show's last for quite some time. The core of the original story is there, though, and it's one of the best and most interesting **Doctor Who** novels.

As we begin the analysis, think back to the opening of *Ghost Light*, where we get a statement of the basic premise at the very beginning. Mrs Grose hustles the day staff out of Gabriel Chase. Night is about to fall, and when Light is gone, the monsters come out to play.

2. 'TALENT BORROWS, GENIUS STEALS': SAMPLING AND REMIX CULTURE

It's not as if *Ghost Light* is the first **Doctor Who** story to have taken elements from previous works. One of the more popular eras of the show, the Philip Hinchcliffe/Robert Holmes years (1975-77[15]), is basically 'Spot the horror movie'[16]. Nor is **Doctor Who** unique in this. All art and works of entertainment take from what has come before to build something new. What I would say sets *Ghost Light* apart from what **Doctor Who** had done before is the sheer number of sources used to inspire characters or events, or quoted verbally or visually. Rather than try to pastiche a particular film or book, it tries to capture an era, taking a lot of small pieces and building something new.

In this, *Ghost Light* reflects something that was gaining popularity at the time in entertainment, and would go on to become an integral part of culture in the modern world. 'Sampling', the act of taking a piece of previously recorded music and using it in a new composition, could trace its origins back to experimental electronic artists and disc jockeys in the 1970s, but its use was really popularised by dance and hip-hop artists in the mid- to late 80s. Those two genres made regular use of snippets of earlier work as a foundation to build on – sometimes relying so heavily that they found themselves in legal trouble as, in those early days, the rights-

---

[15] Specifically, Holmes and Hinchcliffe worked together (as Script Editor and Producer respectively) from *The Ark in Space* (1975) to *The Talons of Weng-Chiang* (1977).

[16] For a more in-depth look at this, read *The Black Archive #5: Image of the Fendahl* by Simon Bucher-Jones.

holders to the original work were not always credited or compensated[17]. What those legal battles really reflect, though, is not a change in how art or entertainment is created. There has always been influence and quotation; what sets sampling apart is the technology. By 'technology', I don't just mean computers, though we will get to that.

The very first forms of art and entertainment, stories told around the campfire after a hard day hunting and gathering, drew inspirations from real-life experiences and the stories that had come before[18]. Every time a story was retold, the person doing the retelling changed something, brought something of themselves to the new story.

The first significant technological change is the written word. With writing it is now possible for the same information to reach multiple people exactly as the writer intended. It introduces permanence and closure. By 'closure', I mean that for the first time, the creator of the work is able to look at it and say, 'It's done.' Works are no longer forced by the method of recreation to be ephemeral and mutable.

Setting the work down allows it to be copied, in whole or in part. Characters used or created by one author can be used by another. *The Epic of Gilgamesh* (c2100 BCE) wasn't created by a single person. No playwright in ancient Greece had a legal claim to use of the gods, but authorship could be established and was accepted for

---

[17] For example, the legal battles over Vanilla Ice's 'Ice Ice Baby' (1989) using the bass line of 'Under Pressure' (1981) by Queen and David Bowie.
[18] Just ask Nimrod.

individual works. Reproduction was confined for a long time to copying by hand, which limited the scope of distribution and thereby influence. The invention of the printing press, and mass distribution of identical copies, was the next great change.

The performing arts evolved along similar lines. Distribution of plays and musical notation, first by hand, then by mechanical means, allowed different performers to offer their interpretations of finished works. The performances themselves, though, would be lost once ended, their only record the memories of the audience, and that record would die with the death of the last audience member. It is a difficult concept to convey sometimes in the modern world, where it seems as if nothing goes unrecorded[19]. There is a Japanese phrase, 'mono no aware', which literally means 'the feeling of things', but what it actually signifies is that things, events, life are transient, and awareness of that transience makes them more special. Even after the invention of recorded media, first audio then visual, there was no guarantee of a permanent record. I suppose that's obvious to a **Doctor Who** fan. Unless you were watching when it was broadcast or something very special happens, you (and I) are never going to see *The Power of the Daleks* (1966).

Even with recording technology, existing works still mostly served as influences or sources for quotation. A character would quote, or a title be taken from a quote, from Shakespeare[20]. A costume, character or a camera angle would be inspired by another film[21]. It was nothing new; technology just made it easier to do, and easier

---

[19] Stop taking photographs of your food. No one cares.
[20] E.g. **Star Trek** (all versions, a lot).
[21] E.g. **Star Wars** (the first one, a lot).

for the audience to detect as it finally became possible through global distribution for everyone to be exposed to the same influences. As a result, it's possible, as you grow up and re-watch your favourite shows, to recognise that the Time Lord in *Genesis of the Daleks* (1975) looks like Death from *The Seventh Seal* (1957) or *The Seeds of Doom* (1976) is *The Thing from Another World* (1951) crossed with *The Quatermass Xperiment* (1955) and *The Day of the Triffids* (1963).

What sets sampling apart, and becomes more prevalent as it was made easier with digital technology, is the use of perfect replicas of the original, and the combining of multiple disparate pieces of other, often wholly unrelated, works to create something new. Artists have become more and more proficient in their ability to do this, to the point that we now have musical acts like Girl Talk that build entire albums of material from samples. While this type of thing is most prevalent in music, there have been similar examples in other media. In books, there has been the re-purposing of classic texts as modern genre books such as *Pride and Prejudice and Zombies* (2009), *Sense and Sensibility and Sea Monsters* (2009) and *Charles Dickens' Martian Notes* (2015)[22]. In television, the recent television series **Hannibal** (2013-15) and **Fargo** (2014-) have taken the creatively, if not always financially, successful tack of fracturing previous works and putting them back together in new and interesting ways[23]. One of the most notable examples outside

---

[22] By Seth Grahame-Smith, Ben H Winters and Simon Bucher-Jones respectively.

[23] Thomas Harris's **Hannibal Lecter** books and their film adaptations in one case, and the entire filmography of the Coen Brothers in the other.

music is in comic books, where Alan Moore's **The League of Extraordinary Gentlemen** series (1999-) draws from such a large list of sources that entire books are published just to explain them all[24].

These are the technologies and concepts that were being explored in the culture in which *Ghost Light* was made; and even after the series' revival – and 10 series produced in a world of mash-up songs and YouTube remix clips – it is still the best example **Doctor Who** has produced. The closest the show came to doing something like this before was *The Five Doctors* (1983) which, as an anniversary special, drew on numerous previously appearing characters[25], and includes a clip from a previous episode which you could count as either a recap akin to 'previously on' or a sample, depending on your frame of mind. But these aren't outside elements the show is throwing together to create something new. *The Five Doctors* is looking inward. It is **Doctor Who** referencing itself, which is all well and good for an anniversary special, but became a bit of a problem in the years that followed, as the show continued to do so and frequently provided diminishing returns[26]. In order to survive, the show has to seek out new life from the outside. Which is a lesson the modern show seems to have learned. When it gathers together that number of returning characters, it tends to use them as set dressing, as in *The Pandorica Opens / The*

---

[24] *Heroes & Monsters: The Unofficial Companion to the League of Extraordinary Gentlemen* by Jess Nevins (2003).

[25] Including, unsurprisingly enough, five Doctors.

[26] For example, *Attack of the Cybermen* (1985) references little outside of previous **Doctor Who** stories, and those elements are there chiefly to provide nostalgia and nothing really new is done with them. This is also a weakness with a lot of tie-in media.

Big Bang (2010), or cameos to establish the global nature of a threat, as in *The Wedding of River Song* (2011). It feels less need to give everyone something to do.

In episode 2 of *Ghost Light,* when Ace finds Lady Pritchard and Gwendoline under the sheets in the observatory, she says 'They're just toys! They're just Josiah's toys.' This is in the same room where the Doctor and Ace initially landed and Ace, in her initiative test, was undecided as to whether they had landed in a laboratory or a nursery, though she 'likes the toys.' Gabriel Chase acts as a big doll house for Josiah, not just full of the people that were there when he arrived (the Pritchards and their staff) and those he brought with him (Control and Nimrod) but those he's invited either deliberately or through his actions (Redvers, Inspector Mackenzie, Rev Matthews, and ultimately the Doctor and Ace). This reflects the fact that the story is a toy box for the makers of *Ghost Light*, who have taken all these characters and images and concepts from other works and set them against each other.

There is an old episode of **The Twilight Zone** (1959-64) called *Five Characters in Search of an Exit* (1961). It's pretty much exactly what the title says. Five people (a ballerina, a major, a clown, a tramp, and a bagpiper) are trapped in a featureless cell. The entire episode revolves around how these disparate types react to each other when faced with this obstacle[27]. At the end of the story, it turns out they are a collection of child's dolls. Their prison is a barrel they've been thrown in as donations to needy children. There are similar narratives – the movie *Cube* (1997) is the first that springs to mind

---

[27] Warning: I am about to spoil this, which will upset some of you even though it's older than **Doctor Who** itself. Too bad.

– that rely on this kind of interaction and that is what *Ghost Light* reminds me of. It is as if Marc Platt is saying, 'I'm going to take this character from this, and this character from this, and this character from this, and then I'm going to put them in a house with the Doctor and shake real hard.'

The closest parallel for *Ghost Light* in all the works mentioned so far is **The League of Extraordinary Gentlemen**. Though **LOEG** came quite a bit after *Ghost Light*, its author, Alan Moore, was one of the principal influences on the stories of Sylvester McCoy's **Doctor Who** run. Script editor Andrew Cartmel gave potential writers for the show copies of Moore's **The Ballad of Halo Jones** comics (1984-86) as an example of what he was looking for, and even tried to get Moore to write for the show[28]. For those unfamiliar – or familiar with it only through the movie adaptation[29] – **The League of Extraordinary Gentlemen** is a kind of superhero team-up book for characters from Victorian literature[30]. Characters from Wells, Verne and Stoker among others mix together in an original adventure. There's an antecedent in Philip José Farmer's **Wold Newton** books, which also postulate a universe where all these fictional characters exist and interact[31].

---

[28] Bishop, David, 'Andrew Cartmel Interview', TSV #40, July 1994. Alan Moore wrote a couple of backup stories for **Doctor Who Weekly** (including *Black Legacy* and the **4-D War** cycle) in 1980-81, but never the main strip.

[29] Which would be a great shame, as that movie is terrible.

[30] In the first two series at least. After that, the scope expanded to encompass nearly all of popular culture, including **Doctor Who**.

[31] There are a great number of **Wold Newton** works, but the core would be *Tarzan Alive* (1972) and *Doc Savage: His Apocalyptic Life* (1973), both by Farmer.

Ghost Light is another bricolage of Victorian literature, but whereas **The League of Extraordinary Gentlemen** takes whole characters from specific works, *Ghost Light* is taking types. The most obvious is Gabriel Chase itself. The haunted house is a fixture of Gothic literature and is such an interesting topic that it gets its own chapter later on. Once you get past that, the first character the Doctor and Ace are introduced to in *Ghost Light* is Redvers Fenn-Cooper. The name itself is a reference to an author whose works may well have been in Gabriel Chase's library, James Fenimore Cooper, chiefly know as writer of **The Leatherstocking Tales** (1823-41)[32], a series of novels about Natty Bumppo, a white child raised by Native Americans. You can see how the name is relevant: **The Leatherstocking Tales** were adventure stories about battles and exploration in the frontier. Yes, it was the American frontier rather than the African one, but the parallels are there.

For Redvers Fenn-Cooper is the very archetype of the British gentleman explorer, beloved of fiction of the era. In his first set of scenes he references Henry Stanley finding Doctor Livingstone, a story that captured the imagination of people at the time and was in large part responsible for the popularity of the type. He also references 'giant dinosaurs' and 'young Conan Doyle' which is an obvious reference to Arthur Conan Doyle's **Professor Challenger** books (1912-29)[33] and implies that Redvers was the inspiration for

---

[32] Beginning with *The Pioneers: Or The Sources of the Susquehanna; a Descriptive Tale* (1823).

[33] Arthur Conan Doyle would have been 24 at the time of *Ghost Light*. His first **Sherlock Holmes** story, *A Study in Scarlet* (1887) would not be published until four years later, and the first **Challenger** novel, *The Lost World* (1912) not until nearly 30 years after Redvers disappeared off the face of the earth.

the Challenger character. Another popular gentleman explorer of the time was Allan Quatermain, created by H Rider Haggard[34]. In fact, the gentleman explorer has appeared so often in various media over the years that you could get away with doing a novelty song about it[35]. *Ghost Light* is not even the first time this kind of character has been used in **Doctor Who**: just a year before, *The Greatest Show in the Galaxy* (1988) had Captain Cook looking even more the type, pith helmet and all, though Redvers proves to be more of a gentleman than Cook.

As a character, Nimrod is a fusion of multiple types. His hunched manner of walking is meant to remind you of the servant character you would see in a Gothic novel or horror movie, like Igor from the movie *Frankenstein* (1931) – except that that character was actually named Fritz and people only remember him as Igor because they are in fact remembering Mel Brooks' parody *Young Frankenstein* (1974). Another aspect of Nimrod's character is the native plucked from his home and brought back to 'civilisation' to serve. Characters like this often showed up in the same kind of fiction as the gentleman explorer. They would serve as the explorer's native guide and prove so useful and trustworthy they were brought home. An example would be the Hottentot Hans from the **Allan Quatermain** books, and the tradition continued as Gothic fiction crossed the Atlantic and transitioned into pulp fiction, with characters such as Tonto in **The Lone Ranger** (1933-54) and Kato in **The Green Hornet** (1936-52) and beyond. Admittedly, Nimrod's native land is a bit farther away than most, and that's one of the

---

[34] First appearing in *King Solomon's Mines* (1885).
[35] 'Hunting Tigers Out in Indiah' (1969) by The Bonzo Dog Doo-Dah Band is just one example.

things that sets him apart from others of the type. Having been separated from it by time instead of distance, he can never go home. No time in *Ghost Light* is given over to Nimrod contemplating how he is the last of his people, but the Doctor will more than make up for that, starting in 2005.

Given the 'native servant' aspect of the character, it is no real surprise that, by the end of the story, Nimrod rejects serving Josiah and Light and seeks advice from, and allegiance with, Redvers. In effect, he is rejecting two genre roles, servant to a mad scientist in a horror story and superstitious native, for a genre role with better prospects.

Sticking with the servants in this piece, we have the juxtaposition of Mrs Grose and Mrs Pritchard. The evil or creepy housekeeper is a standard type in this type of fiction. It's a well-known stock type early enough that Jane Austen parodies it in *Northanger Abbey* (1818). The most well known example is probably Mrs Danvers in *Rebecca* (1938) by Daphne du Maurier. Du Maurier was the granddaughter of George du Maurier, who wrote *Trilby* (1894), which we'll talk about at greater length in Chapter 4. There's also the fact that Mrs Pritchard is the evil housekeeper due to an outside influence, but again that's Chapter 4.

In contrast to Mrs Pritchard, Mrs Grose isn't a character type; she is an actual character from another work, *The Turn of the Screw* (1898) by Henry James. Marc Platt has said that his idea was that after the events in Gabriel Chase, Mrs Grose would find new work at Bly, the house in James's novella[36]. She basically trades one haunted house for another. She performs the same function in

---

[36] Platt, Marc, *Ghost Light* (**Doctor Who: The Scripts**) (1993), p134.

both stories: she is a housekeeper and a handy vehicle for exposition. In *The Turn of the Screw,* it is Mrs Grose who delivers the back story of Miss Jessel and Mr Quint to our heroine. In *Ghost Light,* her principal duty in both of the first two episodes is to tell us that it's almost dark.

Gwendoline is the embodiment of the young girl possessed or manipulated into doing terrible things, trapped in a house of horrors. Examples would include Lucy in *Dracula* (1897), Alice in *The House of Seven Gables* (1851) or Trilby in the novel of the same name by George du Maurier[37]. *Trilby*'s influence on the portrayal of hypnotism in popular fiction is discussed in Chapter 4 and since that is the most important facet of her character, I will leave the majority of my discussion of Gwendoline for that chapter. That said, Gwendoline's chief function in the narrative is as a contrast to Ace. Both are young women who have substitute father-figures in their lives in place of actual parents. Both are being coerced by those substitute fathers, though Josiah's means and end are obviously more malign than the Doctor's. Ace rebels, however, and demands to face her past on her own terms and determine her own path. Gwendoline, whether you ascribe it to the degree of Josiah's control or a fault in her character, accedes to that coercion and pays the price.

There's not much to say about Inspector Mackenzie beyond the obvious. He's comedy relief, a stereotypical portrayal of a British police officer straight out of a skit. He might as well say, 'What's all this then?' when he first walks into the room.

---

[37] And parodied by Austen in *Northanger Abbey* as well.

Josiah fills the role of the mad scientist – another fixture of Victorian and Gothic literature. The most notable examples would include *Frankenstein* (1818) by Mary Shelley, *The Island of Dr Moreau* (1896) by HG Wells, and Robert Louis Stevenson's *Strange Case of Dr Jekyll and Mr Hyde* (1886). There are elements of all of these in Josiah. Nimrod as a hunchbacked, not quite human servant evokes the doctors from both Shelley and Wells. Josiah's own transformation is an inversion of the one from Stevenson's book: bestial to human rather than vice versa. Josiah's wild scientific theories are vehemently denounced, a trait he certainly shares with other mad scientists. (Though I should note that mad scientists' theories are frequently shown to be correct; their failures have more to do with ethics and morals and squishy human emotion[38].) He fits the visual type in his first appearance, with his unkempt hair and dusty clothes. The tinted glasses recall Dr Griffin in HG Wells' *The Invisible Man* (1897). Planning to assassinate the Queen isn't the most ambitious plan ever hatched by a mad scientist, but it does fit into the template of 'I'll show them.' Josiah may see Rev Matthews as just be a toy to amuse him, but he angers quickly when challenged by the Doctor, someone he considers to be close to his intellectual level. This belief in his inherent superiority is a common driver among mad scientists[39].

Gabriel Chase adds to this perception, of course. While the words 'haunted house' are thrown around during *Ghost Light*, it could just

---

[38] Unless they're wrong about the science in a way that causes more disaster.

[39] Note that the other person that angers Josiah the most is Control, as she reminds him of his origins and the possibility that he is not as special as he believes.

as easily be a mad scientist's castle. It's got a (spaceship) dungeon with a cell, a laboratory-cum-nursery, scientific specimens scattered all about the place, and the requisite lightning flashes to add dramatic flair. In the end though, all of this is inverted when we find that Josiah is not the mad scientist, but the experiment.

Where does that leave his creator? We'll get to Light in a moment, but first we should remember Josiah is half of a matched set. Control, like Nimrod, embodies more than one type. In the first couple of episodes, she's the crude creature in the basement, a failed experiment to go with Josiah's mad scientist. The mangled grammar of her dialogue recalls the monster from the film adaptations of *Frankenstein*, or one of the Beast-Men in *The Island of Doctor Moreau*, and one could be forgiven on first viewing for thinking that during the first couple of episodes. It certainly fits with what we've seen of Josiah's interests, and his attitude towards her mirrors that of Frankenstein or Moreau towards their creations, which they regard as failures. 'It's a depraved monstrosity,' he says at the beginning of episode 2, and at the end of that same episode, he calls her, 'quintessence of wickedness, corruption incarnate.'

In the third episode though, Control evolves into another fictional character, Eliza Doolittle from *Pygmalion* (1912) by George Bernard Shaw. No attempt is made to obscure this in the slightest. It is there in Control's desire to be 'ladylike' and Ace using the 'Rain in Spain' elocution exercise to teach Control. I should note that 'The Rain in Spain' isn't in the original play, but was written by Shaw for the film adaptation *Pygmalion* (1938), and more famously used as a lyric in the musical adaptation *My Fair Lady* (1956); and even though it is Ace whom the Doctor calls 'Eliza' in episode 1, it is Control's story that follows the character arc from the original play.

Light doesn't represent a literary type, so much as a fictional device. Light is a literal deus ex machina – and unlike most people, I know what 'literal' means and I'm using it correctly. Light is visually coded as an angel, as Ace points out in episode 3[40], and spends most of the first two episodes in a machine[41]. The Doctor's purpose in having Control release Light is to resolve the plot. Light isn't a very good deus ex machina, though, as he proceeds to escalate the problem rather than solve it. At that point, he does start to resemble something out of Victorian or Gothic fiction, the creation run amok. Here we have another inversion. The true mad scientist, revealed, displaces Josiah – but then behaves like the true monster, because by the end, the role of mad scientist is actually the Doctor's. Light is the Doctor's experiment gone wrong, and the Doctor's responsibility to stop.

All of these character types became so common, so clichéd, over the years that they are better known today through parody or subversion. That's why sampling and remix culture has become such a fixture of the modern world. What do you do with these works of art in a world where everything is available? Where, however great they are, their impact and influence has been thoroughly digested and the state of the art has moved on? You take those pieces and you find a new place for them, through juxtaposition or changing the angle at which the audience views them. You take those old characters types and genres, and you make them evolve.

---

[40] 'It's an angel, stupid.'
[41] 'Angel, not god,' you might say. Nimrod worshipped light as a god. It's close enough.

There are numerous references to other works in the dialogue as well, the most famous being in episode 3 when the Doctor asks, 'Who was it said Earthmen never invite their ancestors round to dinner?' It was Douglas Adams of course, which delights fans since Adams worked on **Doctor Who** as a writer and script editor (1978-80). The actual quote from episode 1 of **The Hitch-Hiker's Guide to the Galaxy**[42] is 'Earthmen are not proud of their ancestors and never invite them round to dinner.' Someone, whose name I can't recall[43], explained to me that this means that *The Hitch-Hiker's Guide* exists in the **Doctor Who** universe, but what he meant was the fictional *Guide*, the book from the show. The quote though, isn't from the fictional book; it's the narrator. The show exists in the **Doctor Who** universe, and presumably the **Doctor Who** universe's Douglas Adams went on to work for whatever show was premiering during episode 2 of *Remembrance of the Daleks* (1988)[44].

There are so many quotes and references in the dialogue that if I were to give into the temptation to list them all and trace out their origins, it would, ironically, strain the definition of fair use[45]. It's not 'List of samples from "All Day" by Girl Talk'[46] long, but it's still long. For example, in addition to all the references previously enumerated in relation to the characters, there are multiple

---

[42] The radio series, from which all else derived.
[43] Sorry.
[44] And Tennant's reference in *The Christmas Invasion* (2005) is to Arthur Dent as a fictional character, and the 'nice man' was Adams. It certainly wouldn't be the first time the Doctor referenced a work of fiction or meeting a writer.
[45] Not to mention the page count.
[46] 'All Day Track Listing'.

references to Lewis Carroll, which should be unsurprising in a series with so many young girls going on strange adventures.

There are visual quotations as well. The bright light emitting from Redvers Fenn-Cooper's snuff box evokes the glowing briefcase from the film *Kiss Me Deadly* (1955) which was also visually quoted in *Repo Man* (1984) and, later, *Pulp Fiction* (1994). Note that the briefcase in *Kiss Me Deadly* contains radioactive material, and the snuff box in *Ghost Light* is said by the Doctor to be 'slightly' radioactive. *Repo Man* predates *Ghost Light*, and even though it's set in the United States, it is by one of the better living UK directors, Alex Cox, so it's not out of the realm of possibility that it was seen by people working on **Doctor Who**. It's also a more likely inspiration, as the glowing car trunk isn't just due to radioactivity, it's due to alien radioactivity.

Another visual quote in episode 1 is Mrs Pritchard's reaction shot to Rev Matthews, which not only references similar stony reaction shots from servants in evil households but, combined with the musical sting, is hilarious. Though this may just be my reaction because it always makes me think of Frau Blücher[47] in *Young Frankenstein*.

There are others, but I want to end this chapter by talking about something you might have thought of already and if you hadn't, you should have. The single outside work that most resembles *Ghost Light* is *The Rocky Horror Picture Show* (1975). Honestly, there are more parallels here than with anything else. Two people, a man and a woman (the Doctor and Ace/Brad and Janet), go into a haunted house full of grotesques and horror-movie caricatures and

---

[47] [Whinny].

36

wired with electronic surveillance[48]. There's a mad scientist (Josiah/Frank N Furter) with a creature (Control/Rocky) in the basement. There's a harridan housekeeper (Mrs Pritchard/Magenta[49]) and a hunchbacked manservant (Nimrod/Riff Raff). There's cross-dressing. In both, a minor character is killed and served as food (Inspector Mackenzie/Eddie). They both have a catchy tune, sung by someone who is cross-dressing. The creature in the basement and the hunchbacked assistant both rebel against the mad scientist, leading to his downfall, followed by a piece of the house flying off into space. It's practically perfect, except you have to fudge a bit to squeeze in Gwendoline as Columbia and Redvers as Dr Scott[50].

Even though this fits so well, I have a more difficult time saying that it is a direct influence. The timing is certainly right, and it is well within the realm of possibility that Platt and the others involved in the production of *Ghost Light* had seen *The Rocky Horror Picture Show*, but as we've seen, *Ghost Light* doesn't really attempt to hide its influences and there's nothing in the **Doctor Who** story that you could take as a direct reference. The two pieces are doing the same thing. *Rocky Horror* is drawing on and parodying the same material as *Ghost Light*, so it's unsurprising that they would take on a similar shape.

---

[48] This is one of the things that is left unclear due to deleted material, but this is the significance of episode 1's repeated close ups of the eyes of the taxidermy animals.
[49] Played by Patricia Quinn, who played Belazs in *Dragonfire*, Ace's first story.
[50] 'Great Scott!'

As I said at the beginning of this chapter, **Doctor Who** has always taken elements from outside work. That has always been at the core of the show. Fans have long extolled the strength in variety of **Doctor Who**, and this process of incorporating outside elements and reshaping them is how the show achieves its variety – whether it means taking pieces or, to put it another way, sampling, from horror movies or adventure novels or even historical events. It's not just the series' greatest strength; it is a crucial part of its essence. It could be argued that the show has been at its weakest when it stops looking outward and feeds on its past. In contrast, *Ghost Light* is **Doctor Who** at its strongest.

3. THE SECRET ORIGIN OF A HAUNTED HOUSE

ACE

> This isn't a haunted house, is it Professor? I told you I've got this thing about haunted houses.[51]

The TARDIS is a machine for travelling through all of time and space, a conceit that has been used to allow the show to pastiche as many different types of story as it can, though there has been a kind of winnowing-down over the years as those making the show tried to stick with what they felt worked[52]. The haunted house story is, however, one that the show, in its initial 1963-89 run, only does once right at the beginning, and not again until right at the end. This is surprising, as there are a couple of very good reasons why this kind of story is perfectly suited to **Doctor Who**.

It's a popular story genre of course. Myths and stories of haunted places date back to tribal times; there's a haunted house story in the *1,001 Nights*[53]. As I mentioned before, one of the characters in *Ghost Light,* Mrs Grose, is taken directly from one of the most popular haunted house stories in literature, *The Turn of the Screw* (1898). Scarcely a year goes by that there isn't a movie released about a haunted house, usually more than one. Last year (2015)

---

[51] *Ghost Light* Episode 1. (All script excerpts from the story use the wording in Platt, *Ghost Light* (**The Scripts**), but formatted in line with standard **Black Archive** house style.)

[52] Go ahead, tell me there wasn't a greater variety at the beginning, right after you tell me the last time there was a story with no fantasy elements other than the Doctor, or a musical.

[53] 'Ali the Cairene and the Haunted House in Baghdad'.

has seen a remake of *Poltergeist* (1982), and Guillermo del Toro's *Crimson Peak*, which isn't just a haunted house story, it's a Gothic haunted house story in the same vein as those *Ghost Light* was pastiching.

The other reason, if we're being realistic, is that haunted house stories are cheap. They need a few interior sets and a small, preferably creepy, cast. They don't require much location shooting, and effects are easier as the lights are turned down. It's for that reason that one of the very first **Doctor Who** stories is a haunted house story. *The Edge of Destruction*[54] (1964) fits the definition of what is called a 'bottle episode' in modern television. A bottle episode is a story that uses only the existing sets and the main cast, usually produced for budgetary reasons, and that was the reasoning behind the production of this story. David Whitaker wrote the script in two days to fill out the initial run with just such monetary restrictions in mind[55].

The TARDIS may not necessarily be a house as such, and at this stage in the series it is still being presented to the audience (via Ian and Barbara's viewpoint) as something eerie and otherworldly, but it is the Doctor's (and Susan's) home, and if anything they react more strongly than the two teachers when the doors start opening and closing on their own (a classic haunted house device) and the clocks start melting. At first, you might think that's the reason behind Susan's hostility and attacks towards Ian and Barbara: she's disoriented, there's some time loss and gaps in her memory. She doesn't know these two intruders in her life all that well, and it's

---

[54] That's what it says on the box. Do not email me.
[55] *The Edge of Destruction* DVD production notes.

natural that her first inclination would be to find them suspicious. There's more to it than that though: Susan is being affected by an outside force.

Ian is not in control when he attempts to strangle the Doctor, but he is clearly under the influence of the same entity that was influencing Susan earlier, which we are later told is the TARDIS, attempting to defend itself and its passengers. Now, this is some time before we're told that Susan has psychic abilities or that the TARDIS has 'telepathic circuits'[56]. It also can't be just sympathy between the TARDIS and Susan, because Ian is affected as well. Looking at the scenes in question, it's apparent that the TARDIS is choosing to influence whoever is closest at hand, which also raises the question of why it would bring in someone else to intervene, rather than taking control of the person it's trying to stop.

These two incidents place *The Edge of Destruction* firmly in the style of the haunted house narrative, almost all of which eventually resort to some sort of spectral influence over the living. There are only so many ways that a ghost or spirit can influence the material world, so things like hypnosis, possession and mind control go hand in hand with the haunted house narrative[57].

Another type of incident common in haunted house narratives is influence over the architecture itself. Sometimes it is something as simple (or clichéd) as blood in the taps or running down the walls, but sometimes this happens in more interesting or subtle ways. In Mark Z Danielewski's *House of Leaves* (2000), the Navidson family first becomes aware of the unusual nature of their house when a

---

[56] *The Sensorites* (1964) and *The Time Monster* (1972) respectively.
[57] See Chapter 4 for more on this.

closet door appears in the wall. When they open it, there's a door at the other end. On further research, Will Navidson finds that the interior dimensions of his house are greater than the exterior ones. This is bound to remind the **Doctor Who** fan of the TARDIS; and on those occasions when the series has decided to spend prolonged times exploring the interior of the Doctor's ship, elements of the haunted house narrative creep in, most notably in *Journey to the Centre of the TARDIS* (2013)[58].

With the style of the haunted house story lending itself so well to the fictional and practical realities of **Doctor Who**, you can be forgiven for asking why there aren't more haunted house stories in **Doctor Who**. In fact, I'd argue that in the initial 26-year run of the show, there are only two haunted house stories: *The Edge of Destruction* right at the beginning and *Ghost Light* right at the end – and we'll see that it's arguable whether *Ghost Light* is even a true haunted house story.

It isn't until Steven Moffat enters the picture in the 21st century that the haunted house becomes a regular fixture in the show. Moffat's vision of the show is definitely a spookier one than Russell T Davies's[59]. Comparing *The Empty Child / The Doctor Dances* (2005) or *The Girl in the Fireplace* (2006) to the stories that

---

[58] It's also worth noting the anarchitects from the **Doctor Who** novel *Alien Bodies* (1997) by Lawrence Miles, living weapons in the Time Lord war that infect and change architecture. A lot of the imagery of the 'War in Heaven' from the BBC books and the subsequent **Faction Paradox** series (2001-) owes more to horror and fantasy, while still trying to keep a kind of science fiction veneer.

[59] 'Spooky' in the technical sense, of course.

surround them shows that Moffat has a vision of the show that isn't quite as brightly lit. It's with *Blink* (2007), though, that Moffat does his first haunted house story. In *Blink*, the Weeping Angels are eventually described as alien monsters – and going by their reception, there's a good argument to be made they are the most popular monsters created during the current run of the show. But think about how they are visually presented in the story. They resemble stone gargoyles. They are not seen to move. As presented, they more closely resemble architectural infestation than monsters, like the topiary animals in one of the most famous 20th-century haunted house stories, Stephen King's *The Shining* (1977):

> 'Staring at the hedge animals, he realized something had changed while he had his hand over his eyes. The dog had moved closer.'[60]

The very next year, Moffat writes *Silence in the Library / Forest of the Dead* (2008), another haunted house story with another alien race, the Vashta Nerada, that is visually presented as an alien part of the environment (shadows) rather than incarnate. Yes, eventually the Vashta Nerada are made more tangible, in the form of the reanimated dead, in order to have a physical form with whom the Doctor can interact and communicate. The same thing happens in the second Weeping Angels story, *The Time of Angels / Flesh and Stone* (2010), where the Angels use a captured victim to communicate with the Doctor. That shift in both these stores, from unresponsive, implacable threat to an entity that can be talked to

---

[60] King, Stephen, *The Shining* (1977), p208.

or bargained with, moves them away from the haunted house narrative.

Once Moffat takes over running the show, the haunted house stories arrive one after the other. We get *Night Terrors* (2011), *The God Complex* (2011), *Hide* (2013), and *Under the Lake / Before the Flood* (2015). There's even a good case to be made in a couple of these instances they are not only using the haunted house narrative template, but are being influenced by specific haunted house stories. *The God Complex* shares some of the visual sensibilities of Kubrick's adaptation of *The Shining* (1980), and *Hide* shares the 70s setting and ghost-hunter character with the same year's *The Conjuring* (2013)[61]. We also get a number of ghost or horror stories which have a stylistic link to the haunted house story, including *The Time of Angels / Flesh and Stone*, *The Curse of the Black Spot* (2011), *Listen* (2014), *Mummy on the Orient Express* (2014), *Sleep No More* (2015), and *Heaven Sent* (2015). This is part of the general change in tone from Davies to Moffat. Some have characterised it chiefly as a darker tone, but it's more a change from Davies grounding the show in a soap-opera pseudo-realism to Moffat's view of the show as fairy tale[62]. This naturally leads to the show being darker[63]. Yes, fairy tales are the stories we tell to

---

[61] Which is, in turn, inspired by the work of Ed and Lorraine Warrens, whose writings were the inspiration for Jay Hanson's *The Amityville Horror* (1977).

[62] 'For me, **Doctor Who** literally is a fairy tale.' (Stephen Moffat, quoted in McLean, Gareth, 'Steven Moffat: The Man With a Monster of a Job', *The Guardian*, 22 March 2010.)

[63] '...and the word "dark" is entirely redundant when it comes to fairy tales, at least until Disney makes a version of them.' (Moffat,

children, but in fairy tales the otherworldly and the supernatural are inherently dangerous to those humans unlucky or foolish enough to encounter them.

At this point, you may well ask how I am differentiating haunted house stories from other kinds of stories in **Doctor Who**? Am I being strict or pedantic in some way? Surely there were lots of haunted house stories in **Doctor Who**?

You're right, of course. There were plenty of times when the Doctor and his companions wandered around a spooky place. But in pretty much all of those cases, the spooky place did not end up being a haunted house. It's a museum[64] or a space station[65] or a lighthouse[66]. The 'haunted house' feeling is in how these stories begin. They use the setup of a haunted house story to create mood, generate atmosphere, but they end up somewhere quite different. They more closely resemble a **Scooby Doo** story than a true haunted house story.

On the off chance you don't know what I'm talking about, **Scooby Doo, Where Are You!** (1969-70) was an animated television show about a van full of teenagers and a dog who travelled a post-apocalyptic landscape of abandoned real estate such as decrepit amusement parks and hotels, investigating the supernatural. The kicker of each episode, though, was there was no ghost. In the

---

quoted in Anders, Charlie Jane, 'Doctor Who's Steven Moffat: The io9 Interview', *io9*, 18 May 2010.)

[64] *The Space Museum* (1965).

[65] *The Ark in Space* and *Terminus* (1983) are probably the best examples of this.

[66] *Horror of Fang Rock* (1977).

original run at least, they never found a genuine haunted house, just a bunch of criminals with a fetish for dressing up[67].

The other way **Doctor Who** appropriated[68] the advantages of the haunted house story was in the so called 'base under siege' story. You can see how this kind of story has the same practical benefits as the haunted house story: a small cast and limited sets. Yet it also gains something that the makers of **Doctor Who**, despite the protestations of Sydney Newman during the early years[69], eventually decided was essential to the show. It has monsters. As the show evolved[70] and historical stories fell by the wayside and producers looked for a way to replace the Daleks or just come up with something to hold the kids' attentions, monsters came to be seen as a fundamental necessity for the show. They were seen as such a necessity that they got crammed into stories where they really didn't make any sense: even in the current run of the show, *Father's Day* (2005) is a good example of a monster being forced in and altering the shape of the story around it. This obsession with monsters is what disqualifies a number of stories that might otherwise fit the haunted house template[71].

---

[67] I know they find real ghosts and monsters in the modern series. I don't care. Don't email me.

[68] Evolved?

[69] 'I hated stories which used bug-eyed monsters, otherwise known as BEMs. I wrote in my memo that there would be no bug-eyed monsters in **Doctor Who**.' (Sydney Newman, interviewed in Auger, David and Stephen James Walker, 'Sydney Newman Interview', *Doctor Who Magazine* (DWM) #141, October 1988).

[70] I know.

[71] The best argument can be made for *Planet of Evil* (1975). The anti-matter monster is invisible, though still tangible. It's the

Ghost Light is another notable example of this. Josiah Smith's husks were added to the story because producer John Nathan-Turner requested them:

> 'I confess that the husks are probably the thing I like the least about *Ghost Light*. John Nathan-Turner asked for lots of monsters in the story...'
>
> [Marc Platt][72]

Much has been said about *Ghost Light* being difficult to understand, or taking repeated viewings to make sense. In preparation for writing this book, I've watched the story numerous times, read the book, read the script, et cetera, and I can say that the husks make the least sense of anything in the story. We're told they are the remnants of Josiah's evolution[73], which by itself doesn't make sense. One has an insect head and one a reptile head. Both are wearing suits like Josiah's. Presumably the suits are part of his form, and only appeared when he started to evolve to fit in Victorian times. Josiah has been in control of Gabriel Chase for two years[74]. So are these the only two forms Josiah has had prior to

---

change of direction into a combination zombie/Mr Hyde story, with all the bestial Sorensons running around, that makes it more of a monster story in the end.

[72] Platt, *Ghost Light* (**The Scripts**), p119.

[73] 'These husks. Old cast-offs of yours, I take it.' (The Doctor, episode 2).

[74] Episode 2:

THE DOCTOR
This is Inspector Mackenzie from Scotland Yard. He was sent here in 1881 to investigate the disappearance of the owner, Sir George Pritchard.

the start of this story? During the course of the story, he creates a third husk which isn't terribly different from his 'final' form. How much does he have to change to leave behind a husk? They're pretty solid for husks, able to restrain or hurt people. Do the new forms bud off? Most importantly, Josiah and Control are supposed to be basically the same kind of creature[75]. So why are there no Control husks left behind by her changes? When the husk's head explodes in episode 3, Josiah immediately starts devolving. So does he have to maintain them in order to maintain his present stage of development? The husks only make sense in terms of their real-world purpose.

What makes a story a true haunted house story rather than one that just uses the style of one to tell another kind of story? First, a haunted house is a particular place: even if it includes the surrounding grounds, it is a limited space with a clear boundary. A house can be spooky because there's a vampire or a mummy in it, but if you leave the house the vampire or mummy can follow you out. The house isn't haunted, it's just a place something spooky calls home.

Second, the house has been tainted or corrupted in some fundamental metaphysical way by previous occupants or events. The house in *The Amityville Horror* (1977) is the site of multiple murders. The Overlook Hotel in Stephen King's *The Shining* and the house in **American Horror Story: Murder House** (2011) compound

---

ACE

But that was two years ago!

[75] One of the biggest signifiers of Josiah's will to escape his origins is the fact he has named himself. Control is named for her function, and as the Doctor says in episode 3, 'the survey is Josiah.'

this by having houses that are haunted causing further horrible acts, that add more ghosts which cause more murders, and so on. Sometimes the corrupting influence does not necessarily stem from the current property but is still tied to that place. In *Poltergeist*, the house is haunted due to it having been built on top of a cemetery.

It is those two elements that lead to what constitutes the standard structure of the haunted house story as we know it. Our lead character or characters arrive at their new place of residence. Small scary things happen. They can be noises, objects moving, voices, etcetera. Small scary things become bigger scary things until our leads fear for their lives, safety and/or souls. During this build up, the leads will research the background of the house to find out what might be the underlying cause of the problem. They find some long-buried or hidden secret and attempt to either soothe the troubled spirits or, more often, simply escape. And it's this last part that for a long time made a true haunted house narrative a difficult fit for **Doctor Who**.

Haunted house stories, like most horror stories, are pessimistic in as much as the best possible outcome is survival. A happy ending for a haunted house story is that the protagonist escapes. That's it. **Doctor Who**, typically, is an optimistic show. There may be costs or sacrifices, up to and including the Doctor's own (current) life, but evil is defeated. Protagonists in a haunted house story are trying to escape. Those in a monster story are trying to win.

Keeping that definition in mind, you're now going to realise that I have been misleading you since the beginning of this chapter, because *Ghost Light* isn't really a haunted house story. It is the secret origin of a haunted house – that part of the haunted house narrative where the protagonist investigates the history of the house to find out what horror is behind the haunting. In *Ghost Light*, the Doctor does this in a way particularly suited to **Doctor Who**: he goes back in time to see it first hand[76]. When we first see it, Gabriel Chase isn't haunted yet. The haunted house story about Gabriel Chase took place before *Ghost Light* starts[77]. It is this inversion of the standard narrative — taking what is typically done as flashback or simple voiceover and making it the substance of the entire story, then in turn taking the standard narrative and making it the flashback — that displays the kind of subversion that can make **Doctor Who** so special.

There is a lot in *Ghost Light* to remind the viewer of haunted house stories, beyond the aforementioned Mrs Grose. The phrase 'haunted house' is front-loaded in the very first scene with the Doctor and Ace. Gabriel Chase itself evokes the classic vision of a haunted house in the vein of *The Turn of the Screw*, all the way up to *The Woman in Black* (2012). There are the establishing shots of Gabriel Chase, from a low angle, looming over the grounds[78], the hidden passages that the night staff are stored in, the secret locked room in the basement, the creepy stuffed animals with glowing eyes, and so on. Gabriel Chase might not be a haunted house yet, but it was certainly built to be one.

---

[76] **Doctor Who** is so well suited to do this that it did it again just last year in *Under the Lake / Before the Flood*.

[77] This isn't true of the novelisation by Marc Platt, where Ace's encounter with the haunted shell of Gabriel Chase is the first thing in the book. (Platt, Marc, *Ghost Light* (**The Target Doctor Who Library**), pp7-10.)

[78] In a later shot, there's are even flashes of lightning. Does it get any clearer?

4. 'WHERE IS MY MIND?': MORAL CULPABILITY AND MIND CONTROL

THE DOCTOR

I could forgive her arranging those little trips to Java...

FENN-COOPER

She was hypnotised, Doctor.

THE DOCTOR

...if she didn't enjoy them so much.[79]

Mind control, in various forms, is practically omnipresent in popular fiction, not just fantasy fiction. If you think about it, it makes sense. The basis of popular fiction is conflict, expressed as subversions of the quotidian. As discussed in the previous chapter, the most extreme examples of this are in horror fiction. The haunted house story is a subversion of place or setting. Even more common than that, though, are the subversion of the body (physical trauma and danger) and of the mind (mind control and mental trauma).

Mind control in popular fiction has one principal purpose: to get good people to do bad things. It seems simple when put this way, but think of all the narrative opportunities this opens up, especially in a serial or continuing series format. If you limit yourself to physical conflict or coercion, keeping the protagonist always on one side of the narrative, then the options get limited fast. There's the option of what in professional wrestling is called the 'heel turn',

---

[79] Episode 3.

when the good guy turns bad. And there's the matching 'face turn' when a bad guy turns good. This kind of storytelling was popularised in modern fantasy television by Joss Whedon in his shows **Buffy the Vampire Slayer** (1997-2003) and **Angel** (1999-2004), and that influence is still felt to this day in things like **Arrow** (2012-) or **Supernatural** (2005-). I'm not saying he originated this – this is a staple of genre fiction all the way back, and you can follow it from its origins through the pulps and comics to modern fantasy television – but it's such a core aspect of the world Whedon created where, for instance, Angel is good and Spike is bad, then Angel is bad and then good again and then bad again, and Anya is bad and then good, and Giles is hiding something and so on, that its influence is plain.

Now the problem with repeated heel/face turns in a continuing story is that they eventually wear thin. The character loses any core values that make them a character at all. The lack of consistency just turns them into a hollow device that acts solely to move the plot forward. They lose any believable motivation for what they do. They also become indelibly morally tainted, whether acting as a hero or villain.

That's where mind control comes in. Do you need one of your characters to betray the others? Do you need to sow disruption by giving someone a deep, dark secret that they have to keep hidden? Do you want your upstanding, righteous hero to kill an innocent person? Then mind control is for you. There are however a few rules, and we're going to circle around and back to them as we talk about mind control, hypnosis and *Ghost Light*.

The first thing to do is narrow the focus, as there are hundreds of **Doctor Who** stories, and a substantial percentage of them feature mind control of some sort. There is possession, prime examples of which include *The Hand of Fear* (1976)[80], *Midnight* (2008), and, from the same season as *Ghost Light*, *The Curse of Fenric*. There's mind control though technology, like the Robomen in *The Dalek Invasion of Earth* (1964) or the earpods in *Army of Ghosts / Doomsday* (2006). But the form of mind control in use in *Ghost Light*, as mentioned numerous times in the story, including the quote that opened this essay, is hypnosis.

Discussion of hypnosis in fiction can get tricky because, unlike possession or earpods, hypnosis actually exists. It's important to keep in mind that there is a long tradition of hypnosis in fiction but that its resemblance to the hypnosis doled out by hypnotherapists is equivalent to the resemblance between real intelligence work and James Bond. Even though there is a divergence between the current reality and its portrayal, most depictions of hypnosis in fiction take their inspiration from the origin of hypnotism.

Franz Anton Mesmer was a German doctor who lived from 1734 to 1815. He promoted the idea of animal magnetism, and not in the way you're thinking of right now. He believed that there was an invisible fluid-like force that flowed through and between all living things[81]. He thought that it was possible to use that flow and direct it to heal or influence people. To do this, he would sit close in front of his patient and stare directly into their eyes while pressing

---

[80] 'Eldrad must live!'
[81] You didn't think George Lucas just made that up, did you?

against trigger spots such as their temples or diaphragm. This procedure eventually came to be called 'mesmerism'[82].

It was a Scottish surgeon named James Braid (1795-1860) who used the term 'hypnotism' for this practice[83]. He threw out all the 'magnetism' baggage from Mesmer's research and focused on using eye fixation inductions[84] to create a mental state in his patients. This is really the beginning of modern hypnosis as practised, and while I could trace all the different kinds of therapy and inductions[85] through to the modern day, there wouldn't be much point, because hypnotism as portrayed in popular fiction is still firmly stuck in the 19th century.

By the end of the 1800s, hypnotism had shown up in works by Edgar Allan Poe[86], Ambrose Bierce[87] and, most famously and influentially, George du Maurier. In 1894, du Maurier published the novel *Trilby*, featuring the character of Svengali. Svengali is a hypnotist and a magician, a pairing that is influential in and of itself as the two professions have continued to be coupled throughout the years. He hypnotises the titular lead character, who is tone deaf, into being able to perform as a popular singer. His methods are similar to those used by Mesmer:

---

[82] For more, check out *Mesmer and Animal Magnetism* (1994) by Frank Pattie. Most other books on him are in German.

[83] He did not coin the word, just this particular use of it.

[84] Focusing on an object, i.e. the pocket watch or jewel or any number of other things you've seen on television.

[85] Binaural beats, confusion inductions, the popularity of self-hypnosis tapes, etc.

[86] 'The Facts in the Case of M Valdemar' (1845).

[87] 'The Hypnotist' (1893).

'Svengali told her to sit down on the divan, and sat opposite to her, and bade her look him well in the white of the eyes.

'"Recartez-moi pien tans le plane tes yeux."

'Then he made little passes and counter-passes on her forehead and temples and down her cheek and neck. Soon her eyes closed and her face grew placid.'[88]

Trilby was a popular book and the name Svengali became a term for anyone exerting hypnotic or sinister influence over another. The purest expression of this kind of character in **Doctor Who** is probably Li H'Sen Chang in *The Talons of Weng-Chiang* (1977). While the strongest influence on that character is likely the **Fu Manchu** novels of Sax Rohmer (1913-59)[89], those were in turn influenced by *Trilby*. Chang checks many of the same boxes as Svengali: hypnotist, magician, and racial stereotype.

That portrayal of hypnosis, including in **Doctor Who**, has remained pretty much the same since. The two characters who have used hypnotism the most in the series are the Master and the Doctor, and they tend to use eye-fixation style inductions.

You could be forgiven for thinking that it's some kind of native ability of Time Lords due to their mental superiority over other races, but we never see any other than these two use hypnosis. Mind control, yes[90]. Hypnosis, no.

The Master seems like he's trying to hypnotise people through sheer force of will. 'I am the Master and you will obey me,' he

---

[88] Du Maurier, George, *Trilby*, p92.
[89] Beginning with *The Mystery of Dr Fu Manchu* (1913).
[90] *The Mark of the Rani* (1985), *The Five Doctors*.

says[91]. The most notable thing about the Master's hypnosis is how often it fails when he really needs it to work. He can't hypnotise Jo Grant (at least, not after *Terror of the Autons* (1971)) or Peri[92]. You could attribute that to their proximity to the Doctor, or maybe some safeguard he implanted in their head when no one was looking, but the Master couldn't hypnotise King Dalios or Sabalom Glitz either[93]. This leads to my first rule of hypnotism in popular fiction: the lower the stakes, the easier the hypnosis. Hypnosis is ridiculously easy in fiction anyway. A real induction can take 15 to 20 minutes in a cooperative subject. Aside from the legal issues that could arise from showing a full hypnosis induction on television, it would slow the narrative down a bit.

The Master's use of hypnosis makes sense though, since hypnosis used to influence is typically seen in fiction being utilised by the villain. It's a subversion of the mind and thus morally dubious. When a hero hypnotises someone, it's usually for some benign purpose, such as helping them recall some important piece of information they can't remember, such as when the Doctor hypnotises Sarah Jane in *The Hand of Fear*, or to get past a guard without resorting to violence, as in *The Sun Makers* (1977).

If the hero does use hypnosis as a form of influence, its very use taints the hero's actions and becomes a reason to question his methods. In **Doctor Who**, this has been more prominent in the modern era of the series, where the grey areas of the Doctor's actions are considered something to be examined. For instance,

---

[91] *Terror of the Autons* (1971) and many more after that.
[92] *Frontier in Space* (1973), *The Mark of the Rani*.
[93] *The Time Monster*, 'The Ultimate Foe' (*The Trial of a Time Lord* episodes 13-14, 1986).

when the Doctor meets young Rupert Pink in *Listen*, he wipes the boy's mind of their encounter[94]. When the Doctor subsequently meets the adult Danny Pink, he's about to do it again and is only stopped by Clara's intervention.

However, the most violent use of hypnosis by the Doctor isn't the Doctor directly tampering with someone's mind, but rather turning the villain's hypnosis against them. In *The Impossible Astronaut / Day of the Moon* (2011), the Silence are shown to control people using a form of post-hypnotic suggestion. This ability is so strong that others can use the susceptibility engendered in a person by the Silence.

DOCTOR:

You straightened my bow tie because I planted the idea in your head while you were looking at the creature.

AMY:

So they could do that to people. You could be doing stuff and not really knowing why you're doing it.

RORY:

Like post-hypnotic suggestion.[95]

At the end of the episode, the Doctor turns this ability against the Silence by playing a recording of the Silence saying 'You should kill us all on sight' during the broadcast of the first moon landing, in

---

[94] The Doctor's mental powers are so great by this point that all he has to do is touch the boy's forehead. Try finding a hypnotherapist who can do that.
[95] *Day of the Moon.*

order to turn the entire viewing population into unthinking killing machines. It's presented as a triumph, and no one questions the ethics of killing the Silence[96] or how many people might be killed while trying to do so. I should also note that even though what the Silence do is called a 'post-hypnotic suggestion', it's closer to straight mind control and its closest analogue is Killgrave's abilities in **Marvel's Jessica Jones** (2015-)[97].

That covers the morality of using mind control. Where things get more convoluted is in regards to the morality of actions committed while being controlled. Throw out the old saw about being unable to hypnotise people to do things they wouldn't do while conscious: a lot of lip service is given to that in popular fiction, but the principle's never followed. If it was, there would be little point to having it in the fiction to begin with. So if we take it as a given that people under hypnosis are being forced to do things they wouldn't otherwise do, how culpable are they?

In *Ghost Light*, we are told that Josiah has hypnotised Mrs Pritchard and Gwendoline. This presumably applies to the rest of the night staff as well[98], but although we see them toting weapons they never get any lines, so no time is spent ruminating on their actions. Story-wise, they're given less depth than the husks. Though

---

[96] Though **Doctor Who** has never shied away from killing the bad guys.

[97] It is very tempting to talk at great length about **Jessica Jones**. It came out while I was putting together this book, and it's 13 episodes revolving around all the issues discussed in this chapter. I could even claim relevance, thanks to David Tennant playing Killgrave. I will try to limit myself, but if these topics interest you, you should watch it.

[98] Except for Nimrod, but we'll get to that.

nominally Josiah has turned Mrs Pritchard into his housekeeper and Gwendoline into his ward, their actual functions appear to be as the warden for his prisoners and his assassin. It's certainly possible that he has had Mrs Pritchard kill for him as well. She's as capable of wielding a chemically enhanced handkerchief as her daughter, but we don't see Josiah call on her to do that. In her first scene, she is feeding her first prisoner, Control, and when we see her next she is recapturing the errant Redvers. You could even view her sedation and transport of Reverend Matthews to the upper observatory as a prison transfer.

Mrs Pritchard may be called the housekeeper, but Gwendoline gets the real dirty work. She has killed her father. She kills Reverend Matthews. She is the one Josiah sends to kill Ace, and I'm sure if he could have used the invitation to get her in, he would have used her to kill the Queen as well[99]. She'd probably be more reliable than poor, broken Redvers. We see a slight flaw in Josiah's control in episode 2 when Gwendoline gets confused. Mrs Pritchard immediately steps in to reinforce order, accusing the Doctor of 'filling [her] head with ideas.' Though it isn't really the Doctor who's been influencing Gwendoline at that point; it's Ace who has disturbed Gwendoline's false reality. Suggesting that Gwendoline try on the male evening wear might be enough of a break in her routine to cause a little wobble.

It is the Doctor who finally breaks Josiah's hold on the women, in episode 3. The Doctor picks up Gwendoline's locket from the floor and shows it first to Gwendoline and later Mrs Pritchard. In both cases, the effect is instantaneous and, honestly, a little odd. We

---

[99] For more on Gwendoline's lethality, see Chapter 5.

don't see any other pictures of either of them around Gabriel Chase and it's quite possible Josiah had all of them removed or destroyed. One imagines Josiah isn't a big fan of mirrors to begin with and has had them removed too, but one presumes they've seen themselves in a basin of water or a window[100]. So seeing one's own reflection can't be enough to break Josiah's hold; it must be the sight of the two pictures side by side, reminding Mrs Pritchard and Gwendoline of their true relationship and what has happened to them.

But the locket hasn't been hidden. Gwendoline was wearing it. We see her touching it. Are we really to presume that she has not looked inside it for two years? Yes, there's precedent. In *The Android Invasion* (1975), Crayford doesn't notice he still has two eyes for two years[101]. I would submit it's the Doctor's presence that makes the difference. As we saw before, he's a powerful hypnotist in his own right, more powerful than the Master (who we're told is a powerful hypnotist), and we're in an era of the show that loves implying the Doctor has a mysterious past with associated powerful abilities[102].

Note that Josiah has only hypnotised the women of Gabriel Chase. When it comes to the men of the house, he takes a different tack. Sir George was killed so that Josiah could take his place as head of household. Nimrod was trained as a servant and kept in line

---

[100] Note how seeing his reflection calms Redvers, though he has not been hypnotised.

[101] Maybe there's a two-year limit on not noticing the obvious in the **Doctor Who** universe.

[102] *Remembrance of the Daleks*, *Silver Nemesis* (1988), the deleted scenes from *Survival*.

through religious fealty, with Josiah as representative of the absent Light[103]. The most notable example is Redvers. Josiah wants Redvers to use his invitation so they can kill the Queen. In more than one scene, we see Josiah reminding Redvers of this and trying to convince him. This is a man that Josiah is keeping prisoner in a straitjacket, but he feels that he needs to talk Redvers into going along with his plan. When Redvers decides to take Control instead, Josiah just gives up. Why doesn't Josiah hypnotise Redvers into doing what he wants? It's either because Josiah is sexist[104] or because the tradition of hypnosis in fiction is sexist[105].

There is the trope that it's more difficult to hypnotise those with 'strong wills', but that itself is sexist considering the context in which this trope is normally found, i.e. adventure fiction with male leads. Josiah has six women bending to his will but he can't control the man whose mind snapped when he caught a glimpse of Light? That's giving Redvers the benefit of the doubt, as well, that what he

---

[103] So he and Matthews have more in common than they'd care to admit.

[104] Which would certainly suit his attempt to embody the Victorian gentleman.

[105] In this the worlds of fictional hypnotism and real hypnotism have in a sense crossed back over. Neurolinguistic programming (NLP) was developed in the 1970s and its techniques have since been used by pick-up artists belonging to the so-called Men's Rights Activism movement. The history of this is long and complex, and there's no good single source I can point you to (other than to say avoid Wikipedia at all costs as it is the battleground for ongoing editing wars). 'The Sociopath Mind Guru and the TV Hypnotist' by Jon Ronson from Lost at Sea (2012) is about the founding of NLP, and 'We Hunted the Mammoth' is a website dedicated to following the PUA and MRA movements.

saw was a glimpse of Light in its pure form, some incomprehensible Lovecraftian monstrosity that makes your eyes bleed and your frontal lobes twitch – because when Light manifests as an angel in episode 3, no-one else's mind snaps. Josiah also doesn't try to hypnotise the Doctor into killing Control for him, opting to try bribing him instead. It never evens occurs to him to hypnotise Rev Matthews and send him back to Mortarhouse College in Oxford to tell everyone how Josiah Smith is a genius who convinced Matthews of the validity of evolution. Admittedly, it was more fun to turn him into an ape and kill him.

In the end though, Gwendoline and Mrs Pritchard are held accountable for their actions while under Josiah's influence. This would seem to run counter to the idea that they were able to be controlled because of their weak wills. If that was the case, surely they would be blameless. The implication of the Doctor's statement quoted at the beginning of this section is that some part of Gwendoline is conscious of, and derives enjoyment from, her actions. He says this after shocking Gwendoline out of her hypnotised state with the locket, and there is nothing to hint that the Doctor is planning any kind of reprisal against Gwendoline or Mrs Pritchard, but their very next scene is the one where Light kills them by turning them to stone. Nimrod protests a little[106], but he's scarcely a viewpoint character. The Doctor's statement carries more moral weight, especially in conjunction with the exchange right before Light appears.

GWENDOLINE:

Mama, I thought you were lost.

---

[106] 'They never harmed you.' (Episode 3).

MRS PRITCHARD:

Oh, I am, my dear. We both are.[107]

This sequence of events implies that Light's punishment, severe though it is, is justified. That the punishment is biblical in nature – being turned to stone by an angry angel – just adds to this. We are being shown that Mrs Pritchard and Gwendoline were susceptible to Josiah's influence due to a flaw in their character, and that that flaw is worthy of being punished. It isn't always like this, though, and there is a dependable rule when reading or watching any kind of serial narrative to determine just how culpable a character is for what they've done under the influence of hypnosis or mind control of any kind. That rule is that a character's culpability for their actions while under mind control is in inverse proportion to their importance to the ongoing narrative[108].

A character who's just around for one story, no matter how inherently good they might be, who has done something bad while under control, is going to have to pay a price for what they've done. They may pay with their own life or the life of someone they love. They may just end up ostracised from their previous life, forced to leave town or lose their job, but they are going to pay. A continuing character (and we're not just talking **Doctor Who** – this applies to all the others like **Buffy, Angel, Supernatural, Arrow**...[109]) who has done something awful while under control will also have to pay a price, but their price is self-inflicted. They will agonise and

---

[107] Episode 3.

[108] I would like you to call this Dennis's Law, because I've always wanted a law.

[109] ...**The Flash** (2014-), **Smallville** (2001-11), **Marvel's Agents of SHIELD** (2013-) and on and on. Seriously, all of them.

punish themselves and brood very photogenically, while those around them urge them to forgive themselves and say things like 'It wasn't really you'. There may also be a redeeming act at the end of the arc to prove to themselves that they're still the good guy, but eventually they get over it.

In the end, Mrs Pritchard and Gwendoline's most punishable sin is that they weren't coming back next week.

5. 'I WANTED TO SEE HOW IT WORKS' II: SO WHERE PRECISELY IS JAVA?

It's in Indonesia, of course. That's not the Java we're talking about though, and I don't mean the plug-in for your browser either. We're talking about the Java that Gwendoline arranged all those little trips to. It's delivered most of the time as a euphemism for killing people. Gwendoline and Josiah send Rev Matthews to Java in episode 2. When Josiah tells Gwendoline that they are sending Matthews to Java, he pours liquid into a handkerchief similar to that which Mrs Pritchard uses to sedate Rev Matthews in the first episode, but when Ace uncovers the transmogrified Reverend in the specimen display case, she reacts to him as if he's dead and he's presented to us as so, with his eyes wide open and perfectly still. When Gwendoline attempts to send Ace to Java in episode 3, Ace certainly believes she is about to be killed.

However, the problem with the metaphorical location of Java starts in the very first scene in which the term is used. It's the scene from episode 2 where Gwendoline is looking at Inspector Mackenzie in the drawer of the specimen cabinet in the study.

GWENDOLINE

It's one of my favourites in the whole collection. It's from Java.

THE DOCTOR

Java?

GWENDOLINE

The Reverend Ernest Matthews will be leaving for Java soon.

After reviving Inspector Mackenzie, the Doctor says that the constable was 'Preserved. Hypnotised.' Is this the exception to the rule of what being sent to Java means? If being sent to Java isn't actually being killed, just being preserved, then hopefully the Doctor went back and got Rev Matthews out of his case before leaving. This leads to a still bigger issue, though, because who are we told over and over has gone to Java? It's the missing (late?) patriarch of Gabriel Chase, Sir George Pritchard.

This act of apparent patricide is the thing that Gwendoline is supposed to feel the most guilt over, but even the story itself is inconsistent on what happened. Here's more of that scene between Gwendoline and the Doctor in the study in episode 2.

GWENDOLINE

Perhaps he will see my father.

THE DOCTOR

Your father? Is he there?

GWENDOLINE

Uncle Josiah sent him there. After he saw what was in the cellar.

But in episode 3, after the Doctor has prodded the mother and daughter to recognise their true identities, Mrs Pritchard says to Gwendoline, 'And then he went away, to Java. You sent him.'

So let's just reconcile the two by stipulating that Gwendoline committed the act itself under the direction of Josiah, thus allowing both statements to be mostly true. It still leaves us with the question of – where is Sir George Pritchard? The implication is that Gwendoline killed him. So where is the body? Josiah doesn't appear to be a man who disposes of a body of any variety. There's not a corner of Gabriel Chase not decorated with a specimen of some kind. He keeps his own discards in the cellar. I realise that it would probably be too grisly for **Doctor Who**, especially during this period of time, to have a scene where they run across Sir George on display in a glass case[110], but it is out of character. The in-story explanation could be that it would serve as a possible reminder to the surviving Pritchards and break Josiah's hold on them.

Allow me a diversion into pure speculation.

How much more sense would *Ghost Light* make if Redvers Fenn-Cooper had been Sir George Pritchard? I'm not saying there's any indication in the story to say that he is, quite the contrary. I'm saying it would make a lot of the elements of the story fall more neatly in to place. It would offer a better explanation of why the house is stuffed to the gills with taxidermy. It would explain why no-one has come looking for 'one of the finest explorers in the Empire.'[111] It would fit in with the way Josiah has transformed the

---

[110] The only reason they get away with it with Reverend Matthews is that the transformation into an ape shifts it into a more fantastical arena.

[111] Episode 1. Though it doesn't explain why no one came looking for Inspector Mackenzie. Did no-one know what case he was working on? And even if they didn't link his disappearance to

rest of the family, Mrs Pritchard into the housekeeper and Gwendoline into his ward. It would explain why Josiah chose to land the ship under Gabriel Chase in the first place.

Having said all that, there is a simple reason why you couldn't do it. It would greatly complicate the end of the story. You can't just have the father fly off into space right after he regains most of his mind but his wife and daughter have been killed. Even in an era of **Doctor Who** less concerned with dwelling on emotional beats, it would just come off as monstrously callous.

So here's the explanation that works to explain the inconsistency in the use of 'going to Java': Inspector Mackenzie **was** dead. The Doctor told Ace that Mackenzie was hypnotised and preserved because Ace has already told him that she doesn't like dead things[112], and she's already creeped out enough by being in Gabriel Chase without being told that the dead walk among us. Late in episode 2 the insects in the upper drawer of the specimen cabinet in the study come alive. It may be a supposition, but I'm going to say that Josiah didn't hypnotise the bugs. In episode 3:

ACE

It's weird, it feels like this whole place is coming alive.

THE DOCTOR

Yes. It's the energy from Light's ship. Invigorating, isn't it?

Gabriel Chase, they assigned no one else to investigate the disappearance of Sir George Pritchard?
[112] Episode 1.

Apparently very invigorating indeed[113].

---

[113] This also fits in with the religious imagery of Light as an angel returning to Earth and the dead rising as a result, but religion is for the next chapter.

6. SCENES FROM THE CLASS STRUGGLE IN GABRIEL CHASE: DARWINISM, SOCIAL DARWINISM, AND RELIGION

Ghost Light is about evolution and, more specifically, about Charles Darwin's theories regarding evolution. At least that's what most people say[114].

Including the official BBC website:

> 'Its themes derive from Charles Darwin's *On the Origin of Species*.'[115]

And including the story's writer:

> '*The Bestiary*, as the story was originally called, is essentially about evolution.'[116]

To get to the truth of the matter though, it's necessary to define not just what evolution and Darwin's theories are, but what we mean when we say a story is 'about' something[117]. Evolution and Darwin are certainly talked about a great deal in *Ghost Light*, principally in the scenes with Rev Matthews and in the final-

---

[114] I could quote a lot of reviews right here, but it would do nothing but pad the word count by having several people all say variations on '*Ghost Light* is about evolution.' So let's stick to the two most important.

[115] Originally from Cornell, Paul, Martin Day and Keith Topping, *The Discontinuity Guide* (1995), p351, republished at 'Doctor Who: The Classic Series: Ghost Light'.

[116] Platt, *Ghost Light* (**The Scripts**), p116.

[117] Defining 'about' sounds ridiculous I know, but bear with me. Why yes, I have studied law.

episode conversation between the Doctor and Light, but I'd argue that these mentions are more surface style than reflections on the actual themes. Text as opposed to subtext.

First, what were Darwin's theories that caused such a stir? *On the Origin of the Species by Means of Natural Selection, or the Preservation of Favoured Races in the Struggle for Life* was published in 1859. Darwin was not the first person to posit the concept of evolution in the scientific community[118]; however, he wrote the book for a general audience. The two new concepts that he brought to the public's attention were common ancestry and natural selection.

Common ancestry is the concept that as organisms mutate and adapt to their environments, the tree of biological life forks and produces several different species. Evolution is not a linear process. It is a branching process. Occasionally limbs die as species go extinct but it is not necessarily a one-for-one trade-off. This is why people familiar with Darwin's theories get so upset when an anti-evolution person starts going on about how they didn't descend from apes, or (my favourite) if humans evolved from apes, why are apes still here?

---

[118] His best-known predecessor in this was Jean-Baptiste Lamarck, whose *Philosophie Zoologique* (1809) suggested a theory of evolution through the passing-on of acquired characteristics, but the idea that species might change over time had been proposed since ancient times.

REV MATTHEWS

> Man has been the same, sir, since he stood in the Garden
> of Eden. And he was never, ever a chattering, gibbering
> ape![119]

Natural selection is Darwin's theory of the process underlying evolution. The idea is that reproduction naturally produces variations in each organism. Those organisms more suited to survive in their environment are statistically more likely to reproduce, passing those variations on to the next generation and so on. Darwin presented this theory at a time before our knowledge of modern genetics. The only comparison Darwin could really use was the practice of selective breeding, as used for example in creating new breeds of dogs, which Darwin described as 'artificial selection'.

Ghost Light is set in 1883. So by the time this story takes place, *The Origin of the Species* is 24 years old. Rev Matthews says that Smith has been publishing papers regarding Darwin's 'blasphemous theories'[120]. Smith would not have been alone in that. Natural selection fell temporarily out of favour as a mechanism for evolution beginning in the 1880s. Julian Huxley called it 'the eclipse of Darwinism[121] and it lasted through the beginning of the 20th century. The literature was rife with people proposing alternatives to Darwin's theories, including theistic evolution, the idea that yes, evolution is real, but only because God made it that way. Reverend Matthews might well have ended up favouring that theory if he

---

[119] Episode 2.
[120] Episode 1.
[121] Huxley, Julian, *Evolution: The Modern Synthesis* (1942), pp22-28.

hadn't been turned into a chimp[122]. But there were other theories being published at the time that are more relevant.

Herbert Spencer is generally credited with extending Darwin's theories to sociology, creating Social Darwinism. In fact, it was Spencer who coined the term 'survival of the fittest'[123] as a term for Darwin's theories. Spencer published work on evolution before Darwin[124], but his view of evolution was substantially different from Darwin's. Rather than natural selection, Spencer believed in Lamarckism, the idea that characteristics acquired over a living thing's lifetime could be passed onto its offspring. Spencer also believed that evolution had a purpose, with a goal to achieve at the end. Does this sound familiar? It should. When you look at what *Ghost Light* is actually about, it isn't about Darwin's theories, it's about Spencer's.

In 'The Social Organism' (1860), Spencer argues that society itself is a living thing and subject to the same evolutionary processes and mechanisms as other living things[125]. The controversy surrounding this is in where this it led Spencer and those who followed him. They used this argument to claim a scientific basis for laissez-faire economics and, on occasion, eugenics. The reasoning was this – and here's where the term 'survival of the fittest' comes in – those most suited to their environment survive to pass on their positive

---

[122] Not a monkey. Monkeys have tails.
[123] Spencer, Herbert, *Principles of Biology* (1864).
[124] Spencer, Herbert, 'Progress: Its Law and Cause'. *Westminster Review*, April 1857.
[125] Spencer, Herbert, 'The Social Organism'. *Westminster Review*, January 1860.

traits to their children. Those not suited to their environment don't survive, and their unsuitable traits die off.

Where this thinking leads is: why should society offer assistance to the needy or healthcare to the sick? Isn't that weakening society by allowing the weaker members of society to keep passing down their defective traits? Also, this means that the wealthy and powerful are wealthy and powerful because they are inherently superior and deserve to be there. In extreme cases, this has been used as an excuse to sterilise the 'undesirable' strata of societies, such as the mentally ill or particular ethnicities. This came to be know as Social Darwinism. You know that libertarian friend or relative everyone has? If you're in the USA, he has a Rand Paul bumper sticker on his car and keeps telling you to read Ayn Rand's *Atlas Shrugged* (1957); if you're in the UK, he reads the *Daily Mail*, admires Nigel Farage and wants to dismantle the NHS. Social Darwinism is the basis of what he believes.

Keep in mind that 'Social Darwinism' as a term was not used by people such as Spencer who proposed and promoted these theories. It was used pejoratively by the theory's critics. It was never even used to describe Spencer until after his death[126].

The theories of Social Darwinism were used to explain why those at the top deserved to stay there. So, knowing what we know of these theories, what do we see when we take a close look at *Ghost Light* and its characters? Let's start with Josiah Smith's 'evolution.'

---

[126] Hodgson, Geoffrey, 'Social Darwinism in Anglophone Academic Journals: A Contribution to the History of the Term', *Journal of Historical Sociology* vol 17, #4.

'When Light's observatory ship arrives on any world, the angel sends out its agent, one half of its survey experiment, to gather data. The survey agent adapts to the environs into which it has emerged to assist its data gathering. Meanwhile, the other half of the survey, the Control, remains unchanged on the ship.'[127]

[Marc Platt]

If we were talking purely biological evolutionary theory, Josiah Smith has already evolved into the dominant life form on the planet by the time *Ghost Light* starts[128]. Yes, he got there by way of lizard head in a suit and insect head in a suit, and he's got one more stage to go to clean up a bit and let his eyes get used to the light, but he's pretty much done. There's also the question, what about Light? Are there some kind of inhibitors in place to prevent Josiah from evolving into the same species as Light? As a matter of fact, you have to wonder – if the Doctor had stayed around long enough, would Josiah evolve into a Time Lord? Perhaps he's limited to life forms native to the biosphere in which he is released.

Josiah, though, doesn't think he's reached the top of the ladder evolutionary-wise, and it's not Light or the Doctor that concerns him. Josiah is interested in class. His goal is to have Redvers kill Queen Victoria and take her place as the ruler of the British Empire[129].

---

[127] *Ghost Light* (**The Scripts**), p117.

[128] Stipulating for the sake of this argument that *Homo sapiens* is the dominant life form on this planet.

[129] Let's take a moment to appreciate that this is a very dumb plan. Josiah may have an interest in science, but he's not that bright. If

Josiah is not climbing the 'evolutionary ladder', as the Doctor calls it in episode 3. He is done with that. He is climbing the socioeconomic ladder. Josiah emerged from Light's spaceship beneath Gabriel Chase. He hypnotised Gwendoline and Mrs Pritchard and had Gwendoline (presumably[130]) murder her father so he could take his place in the household as Gwendoline's 'uncle' Josiah. This automatically gives him a certain amount of status and resources. Unless Sir George Pritchard was already a taxidermist or collector[131], the money to buy the specimens that fill every nook and cranny of Gabriel Chase had to come from somewhere[132].

It is important to Josiah that he keeps his hands clean. Killing is something you order, or hire, the lower classes to do. This fits in with his pride in being a moneyed man. Look at the way he offers the Doctor £5,000 to kill Control, and his offence when the Doctor says he's not interested in the money. In a deleted line, he voices

---

Josiah's plan had actually succeeded, all he would have accomplished is getting himself and Redvers arrested and executed. The Doctor arriving and releasing Light actually places the Earth in far greater danger. But of course, he had to show up and do that so that Light's dispersed essence makes the house haunted, so that Ace gets scared and later tells the Doctor, who takes her back to Gabriel Chase, and here we are as **Doctor Who** bootstraps itself once more.

[130] See Chapter 5, if for some reason you are reading these out of order.

[131] And a mighty lucky coincidence for Josiah if he was.

[132] I imagine there's are some very happy vendors and taxidermists who have profited greatly from Josiah's two-year spending spree. (Unless he bought it all on credit. If so, I then imagine a traffic jam of repo men coming to take it all back.)

his displeasure at the Doctor's refusal: 'How you fancy people despise me, with your doctorates and professorships.'

So, on the socioeconomic ladder where Josiah has found himself, he's near the top. He is the current resident master of Gabriel Chase, patriarch of the Pritchard family, with money and servants, both inherited (the female staff) and one he's installed himself (Nimrod). He is also a jailer, keeping Control in a cell in the basement/spaceship, Redvers in a straitjacket, and the hypnotised Pritchards and staff all in the house against their will. Although it's possible that Josiah doesn't consider himself a jailer but more a zookeeper[133], keeping all these people as representatives of their class or type. Nimrod had already been collected as a specimen by Light, and it would certainly fit with how Inspector Mackenzie was being stored.

LIGHT

'I took you up as the last specimen of the extinct Neanderthal race from Earth.'[134]

First of all, if there's one left, they're not quite extinct. Light finished the job by taking the last one. Second, it's convenient that Light is using Earth classifications to differentiate between species, but that's just something we have to live with to keep this from being needlessly complex. Lastly, how many species did Light take specimens of? We can only assume it's not one of each because of the ridiculous amount of space that would take (although Rev Matthews would probably have you believe that you can take two of each on a boat). Maybe he's like a toy collector that only collects

---

[133] Or a collector in emulation of Light, his personal authority figure.
[134] Episode 3.

the rarities – or, even more so when thinking about Nimrod being the last of his kind, Forrest J Ackerman.

For those who don't know, Forrest J Ackerman created and edited the magazine *Famous Monsters of Filmland*[135]. He had a house he called the 'Ackermansion' with a massive collection of memorabilia that he had collected. One of the things Ackerman liked to collect was the last or final autograph of celebrities, i.e. their last signature before death. He wrote letters and even faxed and phoned the spouse of a dying writer to try and obtain these[136]. I have a pretty good idea what you think of that, because I am thinking it too.

As the real antagonist of the story, Light has one of the greatest petty motivations for destroying a planet ever, up there with Marvin the Martian wanting to destroy Earth as it obstructs his view[137]. He just wants the catalogue to be finished. We're never really given an idea of why Light is going from world to world making these catalogues. There's no indication that there's any authority above Light that has demanded he do it, and if there was, is there any reason to believe that they would come behind him and check his work? He's obviously not getting too much pleasure from carrying out this task, so why can't he just be like everyone else who hates their job and just do it poorly? The answer is it's not a job, it's a hobby. The catalogue itself is a parallel to the research done by the 'gentlemen scientists' common to the era. As anyone

---

[135] One of the first US magazines to feature **Doctor Who** on the cover (issue 155, July 1979). I had that issue when I was a kid.
[136] Brock, Jason V, *Disorders of Magnitude: A Survey of Dark Fantasy* (2014).
[137] *Duck Dodgers in the 24½th Century* (1953).

who lingers around discussions regarding hobbies[138] knows, people take their hobbies far more seriously than their jobs. The only one concerned with the completeness of the catalogue is Light, and thus he is the first **Doctor Who** villain who wants to destroy Earth due to being anally retentive[139].

Back to Josiah, and let's take a moment to look at that first scene he shares with the Doctor and Reverend Matthews. Matthews starts railing against Josiah's theories as soon as the Doctor enters the room and is mistaken by Matthews for Smith[140]. When Josiah does enter the scene, Matthews does not even acknowledge the mistake, which speaks to his entire mindset. He just immediately demands that Josiah account for his theories. Before he can though, the Doctor draws Josiah's attention to the case of mounted moths on the wall. Josiah explains.:

JOSIAH

I recently made a study of these moths. Even in a single species there can be a wide variation of colouring from countryside to town. I'm certain they are adapting to survive the smoke with which industry is tainting the land.[141]

---

[138] A discussion board about a cult television show, for example.

[139] See also the ongoing debate about whether 'anal retentive' has a hyphen.

[140] I imagine Josiah picked his own assumed name and, much like the Doctor, headed straight for the most common one he could find. (As he observes in episode 1, 'I'm as human as you are.')

[141] Episode 1.

This is a reference to the study of the peppered moth, whose change from light-winged to dark was termed 'industrial melanism'. It's considered the first real subject of study for natural selection. The time line has been altered a bit here, as the actual studies linking peppered moth changes to natural selection didn't happen until years later[142], but this is notable as it's the only actual example of Darwinian theory in all of *Ghost Light*, and the scene ends right after this exchange. There's another brief exchange between Josiah and Rev Matthews, but there's not much to it before Mrs Pritchard sends Rev Matthews to sleep with a drugged handkerchief. He will wake up in episode 2, but only long enough to hurl a few insults at Josiah before being turned into an ape[143].

And that is it for the religion-versus-evolution debate. There are passing references to religion, the most prominent being Nimrod's name. Presumably he was given the name by Josiah when being taught English; Josiah would no doubt find it amusing to give a living example of evolution a name from *Genesis*[144]. As brief as this is, *Ghost Light* is one of the few **Doctor Who** stories to address religion – keeping in mind I mean actual religion, not every alien

---

[142] Tutt, James William, *Melanism and Melanochronism in British Lepidoptera*, 1891.

[143] Which raises its own questions. If Josiah is capable of this kind of physical manipulation, why is he resorting to bribery, mind control and pistols elsewhere? It might be that it's a vampiric side effect of Josiah climbing the ladder to his next form, but since this is the only instance we see happen, we have to leave that as a theory.

[144] The book of the Bible, not the band – specifically *Genesis* 10:10. People of my age from the USA chiefly recognise Nimrod as a name that Bugs Bunny calls Elmer Fudd and, consequently, used as an insult to signify an idiot in playgrounds across the land.

being who declares themselves a god (those pretty much come in six packs in fantasy fiction). The parts with Light portrayed and perceived as a religious figure are not what I am talking about; in fact that part of the story is closer to those dime-a-dozen gods. It's in the scenes dealing with Rev Matthews that religion gets addressed head-on. The Reverend Ernest Matthews is dogmatic, opposing any kind of change to the status quo with all his fury and will but with no real arguments to speak of. He just asserts that evolution is wrong and Josiah is a terrible person, the latter of which is true, just not necessarily for the reason that Rev Matthews believes. As portrayed, Rev Matthews makes for a decent representation of religious orthodoxy.

Here I'm forced to admit that I was born and raised in the United States of America[145]. As such, when I first saw the scenes between Matthews and Josiah Smith and the Doctor, it was so refreshing to me. No American series, and certainly not one intended for a family audience, would address the 'debate' over evolution in such a manner. Rev Matthews is treated as a comedic figure, a relic of a dying time making his final futile grasps for relevance. The debate over evolution is over and men like Matthews lost. It's telling that when **Doctor Who** does a story with the religion-versus-evolution debate it has to be done as a period piece[146]. It would just seem silly to have it as present-day debate set in the UK. Does it irritate me slightly that a decades old **Doctor Who** story deals with matters of science more maturely than anything that could be found on

---

[145] Yes. I know something so shameful should be kept a secret, but I value honesty when speaking to you.
[146] In the US, we get to experience this debate every election cycle.

television, not to mention politicians and textbooks, in my country? Of course it does.

JOSIAH

The Reverend makes such a tedious toy, don't you think?

GWENDOLINE

Dear Uncle.

JOSIAH

We're so glad he has to go.[147]

Josiah is not the only one in Gabriel Chase capable of transforming himself, though. He's part of a matched pair. When *Ghost Light* begins, Control is being kept in a cell. Mrs Pritchard brings dinner and a copy of *The Times*. The paper is Josiah toying with Control, mocking the bestial prisoner with civilised ritual, but it's probable that this exposure to the world at large in the form of the paper, in addition to the regular exposure to Mrs Pritchard and the servants, is what triggers the beginning of Control's own metamorphosis. That regular exposure to Mrs Pritchard and the servants also explains why Control's changes lead to the form of a human female. I can't imagine that the two entities in their original form had gender identities[148].

Control's evolution certainly takes place at a faster pace than Josiah's. It's taken Josiah two years, while Control's metamorphosis

---

[147] Episode 2.
[148] The only pronoun used for Control until the end of episode 2 is 'it', and her voice is electronically treated to disguise her gender until late in the story as well.

takes place over a single day[149] and without the need for husks[150]. Once Control has escaped her cell and subsequently the cellar, what does she express as her goal over and over? She wants to be 'ladylike'. She tries on clothes. She gets quick elocution lessons from Ace, and her big victory over Josiah at the final dinner scene is getting Redvers to take her to see the Queen. So, like Josiah, her goals are not Darwinian evolutionary goals (especially since Darwinian evolution doesn't have goals) but Social Darwinian goals. Josiah and Control are climbing the social ladder, not the biological one.

Allow me a small aside regarding the costuming of Light's crew. When we first see Josiah in episode 1, there's what appears to be dust and cobwebs on his jacket, or at least that's what the Doctor thinks[151]. But in episode 2, when that version of Josiah has been discarded, it's found by Ace and Mackenzie in the observatory under a dust cloth. You could think that this has been done solely because it's a now-discarded husk, but Gwendoline and Mrs Pritchard are under the drop cloths as well and the implication is there in the scene that this is done every day while they wait for night to return. Also, the previous husks are in suits. Admittedly, it would be distasteful for a Victorian gentlemen to leave his discarded husks laying about the house naked, but then there's Control.

---

[149] Episode 1 starts at 6pm the first day. The climactic events of Episode 3 take place shortly after 6pm the next.
[150] Possibly because Josiah has already marked the metaphorical path for her?
[151] 'Dust to dust.' (The Doctor, episode 1).

Control's appearance changes in close to every scene she appears in, from the ragged monster at the beginning to properly ladylike at the end. And though there is a scene in episode 3 where we see her looking in a mirror and trying out clothes, there's no opportunity for such scenes to take place off screen earlier in the story. The clothes are in fact part of Control's and Josiah's biology, and evolving with them. The decay on the jacket in episode 1 is the jacket itself decaying, and the first warning sign that Josiah is about to change form again. (This also means that Control and Josiah are essentially naked throughout the entire story. Remember this the next time you are watching the scenes with Josiah leering over Gwendoline.)

Josiah and Control are the most obvious examples of evolution in the story, but they are not the only ones from the survey ship evolving due to the events in Gabriel Chase. There's Light as well. As the Doctor points out in his final conversation with Light, 'But you evolve too, Light.'[152]

We're told that Light is a leader of a survey ship, which would ordinarily imply that he's a scientist of some kind, but when he's presented to us it is as a religious figure. Nimrod worships him as a god. His design is inspired by religious artwork[153]. At one point, the idea was to present Light dressed as a vicar with bare feet[154]. In the

---

[152] Episode 3.

[153] '…I added metal feathers to the arms as a further pre-Raphaelite reference, like one of the great Rossetti angels.' (Costume Designer Ken Trew, quoted in Platt, *Ghost Light* (**The Scripts**), p10.)

[154] 'Then, perversely, I thought of a tall and sepulchral figure in a cleric's black cassock – dry and officious, like a bare-footed Biblical accountant.' (Platt, *Ghost Light* (**The Scripts**), p117.)

great religion-versus-evolution debate, Light is firmly on the side of religion, because Light is a terrible scientist. He's not interested in empiricism or testing results. He wants to index everything, like the priests who tried to figure out how old the earth is by adding up all the ages in the Bible.

In my teens, I worked in a used book store. The owner spent most of his days recording dozens of television shows. He would transcribe the end credits into a notebook and cross-reference the credits. The thing is, he never watched the shows. He wasn't interested in the content, just the list. That's Light. (I can only assume that the owner eventually transformed into digital bits and is now known as IMDB.)

Which brings up a question: is Josiah's aversion to light (with a small 'l') truly biological before his final metamorphosis? It's implied. He only comes out at night. He physically recoils from sources of bright light, but the tone of voice he uses when reacting to a sudden exposure to bright light is the same as when he speaks of Light (with a big 'L'). His aversion may not be entirely psychosomatic, but there is little doubt that the association adds to his discomfort. On a subtextual level, Josiah getting over his issues with light could be seen as evolution (as represented by Josiah) finally moving out of religion's (as represented by Light's) sphere of influence.

The Doctor may say Light is evolving, but Light, as evidenced by his denials, views it as a devolution[155]. Light has started as the ultimate

---

[155] Appropriately enough calling it that is, in itself, more in line with the Victorian view of evolution as a process that has an end point, direction or goal. In modern terms, all change is evolutionary, and

authority figure: a god, above Queen, the gentry, and all else. Those who respected his place in the scheme of things turn away during the course of the third episode. Nimrod rejects him in favour of his home[156]. Josiah's first instinct on Light's return is to have one of his servants attempt to kill him. The reason that Josiah and Control hate Light is obvious. He basically treats them as slaves. Control was a prisoner of Light's before she was a prisoner of Josiah's; and Josiah, as he was created to do, is mimicking the highest form of life around (Light) by continuing to keep her so. He also wants to prevent her from evolving and contesting his position at the top of the ladder, and she serves as a constant reminder of his humble origins.

Light was devolving even before this, though. Light's downfall has started the first time we set eyes on him. His manifestation as a glowing angel type thing isn't Light in its purest form. Remember, it was finding Light in the basement that drove Redvers insane: 'Burning bright, in the heart of the interior. It burnt through my eyes into my mind.'[157]

So insane, that just looking at the bright light from the snuff box causes him to scream in terror[158]. Yet when Light shows up at the

---

devolution is a concept really only used in popular culture, for example by the band Devo ('Are We Not Men? We Are Devo!' (1978)).

[156] 'I'm sorry, sir. My allegiance is to this planet.' (episode 3).

[157] Episode 1.

[158] Which leads to one of the big unanswered questions. To quote the movie *Seven* (1995), 'What's in the box?' Seriously, there is nothing approaching an answer to this in the whole story. The only thing we're told for sure is it's slightly radioactive. So is a watch with a radium dial. There is a nice inversion here though, as

dinner scene, Redvers doesn't react at all. Neither does anyone else. This is obviously a lesser form than the one that drives men mad on sight and inspires worship. The fact that Light is devolving is ironic, in that devolution was his original solution to the problem of Earth, as beta-tested on Inspector Mackenzie, 'the cream of Scotland Yard.'[159] He also replicates his solution to the Pritchards – calcification – as he attempts to halt the changes in himself which the Doctor pointed out. As the Doctor says in episode 3, 'File under Imagination, comma lack of.'

The interactions we see between the survey ship's crew are more a model of Social Darwinism than biological natural selection. Remember, it's Social Darwinists who came up with 'survival of the fittest', and part of that concept that you hear from the people who believe in this stuff to this day is the idea that evolution has 'winners' and 'losers'. For something or someone to succeed, another must fail. This is why Josiah thinks Control and Light need to be locked away. With them around, he can't be on top. And we're shown that he is right. Control gets outs, she frees Light, and by the end he's in chains.

It's only the survey team that undergoes physical metamorphosis during the course of the story, but when you start viewing this as a story built around Social Darwinism, an entire hierarchy of social

---

Redvers has been driven mad by the presence of a higher being and that higher being is in turn driven mad by the collective shifting masses of lower beings.

[159] This is the single best joke in a very witty script, and funnier than any of the mugging and hamming it up during other supposedly funny serials of the show. (You know what I'm talking about. Don't pretend you don't.)

dynamics emerges revolving around ambition and class. Now, as a resident of the United States[160] I know that I am never going to get all the complexities of the treatment of class in the UK. You're just going to have to bear with me as I simplify it.

At the very top, we have God, or at least his representative in *Ghost Light*, Light. Beneath that we'll have the Crowned Saxe-Coburg: though she may not be actually present in the story, her presence is surely felt. The next class below that are the titled. That would include Lady Pritchard, her daughter Gwendoline, and (as a Time Lord) the Doctor. We have authority figures in Rev Matthews and Inspector Mackenzie – Redvers probably falls in this category as well. We never find out a great deal about his background, but he's got enough status to get an invitation to meet the Queen. Then there's everyone else, be they Josiah and Control trying to claw their way up or those who are just trying to survive like Ace, Nimrod or Mrs Grose.

As I showed before, in episode 3 Light falls from his lofty perch and becomes a fallen angel who is going to destroy the Earth with a 'firestorm'[161]. Our chief visual representation of royalty, the picture of the Queen, literally has a target drawn on her by the ambitious lower class as personified in Josiah. Lady Pritchard has been brought low and made to serve. Gwendoline is corrupted by her association with Josiah, a relationship which is presented as unsavoury even beyond her role as his chosen assassin. Look at Rev Matthews' final scene with Josiah in the upper observatory. Josiah

---

[160] I know. I'm sorry.

[161] More than a little William Blake here. 'Lucifer' means 'light-bringer' after all.

is creepily sexual towards Gwendoline[162] and Matthews reacts to this: 'You're no better than animals.'[163] Identifying the lower classes as sexually promiscuous or predatory, especially towards their 'betters', has frequently been used to justify why they need to be controlled, segregated, or even sterilised, which circles back around to eugenics and how it derived its justification from Social Darwinism.

Next is the Doctor. He is titled, a Time Lord after all, but he is not treated as such in the story. As the show has told us, the Doctor fled his inheritance, or at least what his people regard as his inheritance. Nowhere in *Ghost Light* is the Doctor called a Time Lord. This may not seem that unusual but in the '80s, 'Time Lord' was practically used as a pronoun for the Doctor, so we can view its absence as significant. Not only that, but Ace's habit of calling him 'Professor' fits the way he acts in this story. He starts the story testing Ace, attempting not just to educate her, but as better teachers do, to teach her how to learn on her own. When he interacts with Josiah and Rev Matthews, it is as a scholar; he interacts with Redvers as an explorer. When it is revealed that he has brought Ace back to Gabriel Chase to deal with the trauma she had as a (younger) child, he is once again the Doctor, though this is one of the few times the title 'Doctor' could be thought of to refer to him as a therapist.

Our authority figures in *Ghost Light* are uniformly awful. I talked about Rev Matthews before while discussing Light. He could be considered a straw man if he wasn't so accurate. There's not much

---

[162] Or sexually creepy, you can pick.
[163] Episode 2.

good to say about Inspector Mackenzie either. He's not smart or observant, or terribly good at his job. Admittedly, he's not on screen for a great deal of time and in that time all we really know about him is he's hungry and he's racist: 'Gypsy blood. I can see it in him. Lazy workers.'[164]

Libertarians[165] who believe in Social Darwinism would appreciate the fact that both our authority figures in *Ghost Light* are so ineffectual. Authority, particularly government-derived authority, is seen as a force that prevents the truly great from achieving success. But that's not why they are presented so here. It is actually necessary to the structure of a **Doctor Who** story. How many stories would be over in about five minutes if the authorities were doing their job?

In terms of Social Darwinism, Redvers certainly works as a representation of colonialism and imperialism. He is, after all, 'one of the finest explorers in the Empire,' even if the person who calls him that is Redvers himself[166]. As an explorer of that period, what would he do? He would travel to other 'less civilised' places, trade with the natives, search for rare, exotic beasts, and shoot them. Which is exactly how his damaged mind is interpreting the events in Gabriel Chase. We're told that Josiah has invited Redvers to Gabriel Chase and kept him prisoner because he wants Redvers' invitation to meet the Queen, but there's more to it than that.

---

[164] Episode 2. Don't try to excuse this by saying he is a product of his time. It's true. He is a product of his time, his racist, sexist, classist time.

[165] And just as a reminder, I mean the Ayn-Rand-descended, predominantly US strand of libertarianism.

[166] Episode 1.

Redvers also describes himself as Josiah's 'sternest opponent.'[167] Josiah invited Rev Matthews to the house to toy with him as revenge for his public criticism of Josiah. It has to give Josiah a bit of added pleasure to take another opponent, also of higher stature and practically an embodiment of imperial values, and use him as a weapon against the Empire.

There are a lot of servants in *Ghost Light*. If you count Mrs Pritchard, and I am for the purposes of this sentence, they make up nearly half the cast, if only three speaking parts – those being Mrs Pritchard, Mrs Grose, and Nimrod. Mrs Pritchard is formerly Lady Pritchard, and it shows that Josiah has truly inherited the attitudes of a privileged wealthy white male as he doesn't see her as enough of a threat to send to Java along with her husband.

Mrs Grose is, as discussed in Chapter 2, just a reference to another story. Her chief narrative function in both of her scenes is to tell us it's almost dark and hurry the rest of the day staff out the door.

The night staff might as well be automatons for the way they are treated. They're kept in the cupboard when not in use and when Light decides to dismantle one, it's peculiarly bloodless, though this is probably down to the requirements of the time slot as opposed to any fictional significance. This treatment of servants as window dressing is necessitated by the needs of the story, and with the possible exception of Mrs Grose, at least no attempt is made to make us feel okay about it. I have to admit that I just can't watch things like **Downton Abbey** (2011-15) or, for that matter, *Gone with the Wind* (1939), where servants are presented as existing solely for facilitating the life-changing events of the privileged. My

---

[167] Episode 1.

principal reaction to the spoiled daughter of a slave-owner being left destitute is 'good.'

Which, in terms of the servants, leaves us with Nimrod.

Josiah has removed Nimrod from his 'quarantine cubicle,' dressed him up, taught him English, good manners and how to perform the duties of a butler, and presumably helped him get past the trauma of being the last Neanderthal and abducted by a space god. Josiah has many character flaws, but you can't accuse him of laziness.

It would be easy to see Nimrod as being coded in racial terms. There are the lines from Inspector Mackenzie, but he is presented as a dullard and not to be taken seriously. This is also a story that specifically brings up racism in Ace's account of the fire-bombing of Manesha's flat in episode 1. While it is unfortunate that a story that deals with racism, however momentarily, doesn't have anyone in it who isn't white[168], we're not talking about *The Talons of Weng-Chiang* or *The Tomb of the Cybermen* (1967) here. There was a very real tradition of men from the upper classes bringing back natives as servants when returning from military or other overseas service, and that tradition has been reflected in fiction for just as long and could be seen as the antecedent of the much-discussed modern 'magic (ethnicity of choice)' trope.

Nimrod's true purpose, though, is to serve as a living example of evolution in action. We are told that he is the 'last specimen of the

---

[168] *Black Orchid* (1982), another Gothic story in an upper-class household, manages to fit in a non-white character, though in the process it engages in that odd practice where non-white races are seen as interchangeable, in this case a Native American played by an Indian.

extinct Neanderthal race' by Light in episode 3. There's still a fair amount of discussion about what precisely happened to Neanderthals[169], but the implication of natural selection is that they weren't as suited to the environment as *Homo sapiens sapiens* and so died out. Josiah's metamorphosis is explained as an example of artificial induced evolution. What Josiah has done with Nimrod could be seen as an attempt to replicate that, though he's never going to raise Nimrod high enough to be a threat to his own status. Josiah's fascination with evolution might just be an attempt to understand his own origins and the mechanism that he hopes will place him at the top.

Finally, there's Ace. It's in her dealings with the inhabitants of Gabriel Chase that we really see these social dynamics at work. When Ace was first introduced in *Dragonfire* (1987) she was working as a waitress. She was bright, but had been expelled from school. She's presented as a juvenile delinquent. The Doctor tells her that the trip to Gabriel Chase is an initiative test as part of his ongoing attempts to educate her. It's not the first time the Doctor is presented as attempting to educate Ace[170], and at this point we're not told of any specific goal that he may have in mind. The eventual intention was that the Doctor was going to drop her off on Gallifrey to train as a Time Lord[171], but that intention never had a chance to make it to the screen.

---

[169] A good summation with pointers to more in-depth discussion would be Harvati, Katerina, 'What Happened to the Neanderthals?'
[170] He is, after all, the 'Professor.'
[171] Owen, Dave, '27 Up', DWM #255, August 1997.

Ace is one of the wolves of Fenric[172]; her hometown has a portal to another dimension[173] in addition to having hosted an alien spaceship over 100 years previously; and she was transported across the universe by a time-storm in her house[174]. In other words, she is a representation of a typical teenager as they exist in the **Doctor Who** universe, where alien visitations are a weekly occurrence. For her part, Ace is doing what all teenagers do. She's trying to create her own identity apart from her parents and surroundings. The best the Doctor can hope to do, and what he is attempting to do, is influence the outcome so that identity is a positive one rather than a destructive one – or at least to ensure that the destruction is positive[175].

When we first see Ace in *Ghost Light*, it is in the context of being brought to the highest point of a wealthy person's home by a slumming Lord. Which leads to another digression. There's another way that this hierarchy is communicated to the viewer: architecturally. When at rest[176], Josiah, Gwendoline and Mrs Pritchard are in the upper observatory. This is also where the Doctor and Ace first arrive in the TARDIS. They find Redvers upstairs. Control is locked in the basement, and that also appears to be where Nimrod spends the majority of his time. Rev Matthews spends most of his time on the ground floor and is only invited to the upper observatory in order to be killed. A lot of the story

---

[172] *The Curse of Fenric.*
[173] *Survival.*
[174] *Dragonfire.*
[175] 'Wicked.'
[176] If that's what you want to call sitting motionless under a dust cover.

involves characters moving from floor to floor in the house, frequently in conjunction with their change in status relative to those around them. Control first rises in station by escaping the basement for the ground floor. Her next step is taken when she goes upstairs and encounters Redvers. When she fears a setback, she jumps out the window back down to the ground. The only real exception to this is in the final moments when she returns to the basement with Nimrod and Redvers, but that is only momentary because, with her new status, she rises again, taking the entire basement with her this time. It would be a beautiful metaphor about lifting the entirety of the oppressed classes, if I thought there was the slightest chance it was intentional.

ACE

It's a laboratory. Well no, it could be a nursery, but the kids'd have to be pretty advanced. And creepy.[177]

Getting back to Ace, after looking around the upper observatory, the Doctor follows her into the hallways of Gabriel Chase to continue her education – and let's remember, during the time period in which this is set, a woman of Ace's social status wouldn't be educated at all. She could look forward to a life of menial labour or getting married and probably dying in childbirth. If a woman had a higher social status, she would receive some education in terms of literacy or perhaps the arts (playing the piano for example) but even that was mostly to make her more suitable for being an upper-class spouse[178]. Ace's first encounters with Redvers and Rev

---

[177] Episode 1. This is the best description of the entirety of Gabriel Chase in the whole story.
[178] And then dying in childbirth.

Matthews are both marked by their offence at her impropriety. It's an amusing bit of fun on the surface ('Oh look how stodgy those Victorians were') but there's more to it than that. These are wealthy men offended by a young poor woman's entry into their world without properly obeying the rules that generations of wealthy men have set up for society. Josiah's lack of interest in Ace's lack of propriety is one of the things that sets him apart as 'other', and a pretender to the title of gentleman. Neither Nimrod or Mrs Pritchard comment on Ace's outfit when they come to re-capture Redvers[179].

Speaking of outfits, it's interesting to note how the character arcs of the three chief female characters are reflected in their costuming. As I mentioned before, the events in *Ghost Light* take place in little over a day. None of the male characters changes their clothes in this time. Josiah gets a little cleaned up towards the end and Redvers briefly gets an overcoat with very long sleeves that tie in the back, but it's Ace, Control and Gwendoline who get the major costume changes. Ace starts in her modern street clothes. When the Doctor sends her off with Gwendoline to get more 'appropriate' apparel in episode 1, Ace rebels against the Victorian strictures and talks Gwendoline into joining her in trying on gentlemen's evening dress[180]. This doesn't cause that much of a stir in Gabriel Chase, because everyone is so busy running around. Josiah seems more amused by it then anything else. Mrs Pritchard accuses Gwendoline of dressing like a 'music hall trollop' in episode

---

[179] Though I imagine Mrs Pritchard would have, if she wasn't being hypnotised into thinking she's a servant.

[180] Why Gwendoline had not one, but two men's suits in her room I have no idea.

2, but she seems more angry at Gwendoline's mind control starting to slip than any inappropriateness in the outfit itself. They're probably both programmed to reinforce each other's programming when cracks start to show. Finally Ace ends up in the summer dress that the Doctor presumably told Mrs Grose to select, knowing full well Ace isn't going to pick out a dress if he gives her a chance like before. Yes, it's paternalistic[181], but he's the Doctor, so what did you expect?

By comparison, Gwendoline's costume changes are relatively simple. Apart from the brief diversion in the men's suit, she wears a white dress when she is trying to play innocent host, and she wears a dark dress when she's going to run around killing people. The men's suit could almost be seen as a transitory phase where she's wearing white and black together, and it's in this suit that she has her big moment of conflict and doubt. It's also an inversion of Ace's costume changes, where she ends the story in a light dress.

Control's costume changes fall along the same lines but are more gradual to reflect her 'evolution', along with the gradual change in her voice. Control starts out as just a hunched figure in dirty rags. Every time we see Control over the course of the story there are fewer and fewer rags covering the figure underneath. We even see Control removing one of the rags and discarding it in the scene where she introduces Light[182].

Redvers and Rev Matthews would like to see Ace act like a 'proper' young woman, something she really has no interest in being, in

---

[181] Though not third Doctor level of paternalistic.
[182] At the end of episode 2, and recapped at the beginning of episode 3.

either dress of comportment, which makes it ironic when Control turns to Ace to teach her to be 'ladylike'. This isn't a new factor in her life, either. She's had issues with the expectations of authority figures in her life, including her mother[183]. In episode 3, she tells the Doctor, 'You're not my probation officer' and she doesn't say it in the manner of someone who has never had one[184].

Even if he sees it as more of an educational experience, the Doctor falls into the role of the upper-class white male trying to direct Ace's behaviour. He has decided that Ace needs to confront her past for her own good, and when she finds out she calls him on the fact.

THE DOCTOR

We all have a universe of our own terrors to face.

ACE

I face mine on my own terms.[185]

They push against each other until the breakthrough in the third episode when the Doctor finally gives up asking about her past. He says, 'What happened here in a hundred years' time is none of my business', and offers her the key to the TARDIS. It's only this acknowledgement of her agency that allows her to quit running and confront the past on her terms. Unfortunately, she's

---

[183] *The Curse of Fenric.*

[184] This raises the question: did she get caught burning down Gabriel Chase, or was the probation officer from something else, like the classroom explosion mentioned in *Dragonfire*? We never find out.

[185] Episode 1.

immediately separated from the Doctor as Gwendoline tries to kill her. The dynamic changes by the end, though. In the final scene, the Doctor asks Ace if she has any regrets about her previous behaviour and her only one is that she didn't go far enough. The Doctor agrees. His actions towards her are set in a new light. Rather than attempting to change who she is, he has helped her understand why she has made the choices she has in the past, and supports them.

What the Victorian setting of *Ghost Light* does is bring these issues to the fore by taking us to an era where those in power are completely unapologetic about their biases and how they're used to keep them at the top of the socioeconomic ladder. Modern conservatives love to talk about 'PC culture gone mad', to the point where it has become something of a joke[186], but keep in mind that what they're complaining about isn't that they are no longer on top[187]. It's that they can no longer be horrible to other people without those people calling them out for it. They long for a day when people 'knew their place', and *Ghost Light* takes us back to a time when that was very much true – but scientific discoveries were making it harder for those in power to claim that their status was due to divine right or the like. They were already co-opting the language and ideas of Darwin and evolution to come up with new reasons for them to keep their place at the top of the heap.

---

[186] A not very funny joke, considering the Republican obsession with the 'political correctness' in the current US Presidential Election.
[187] Because despite their protestations to the contrary, they still are.

7. 'I WANTED TO SEE HOW IT WORKS' III: GOD'S AWAY ON BUSINESS

Ghost Light is a story concerned with the origins of things: the origin of a haunted house, the origins of Ace's trauma, the origin of religious imagery, and *The Origin of Species*. The story it replaced, 'Lungbarrow', would have been about the Doctor's origins. The story itself is an origin in the sense that it is the model for **Doctor Who** as it is now.

I have to end on this note. There can be an element in analysis such as this that affects the ability to enjoy the thing being analysed: 'knowing how the sausage is made' if you will. I chose to do this book on *Ghost Light* for the opportunities that the complexity and depth of the story afforded, but also because I simply enjoyed the story[188]. It pleases me to report that after spending about a half a year thinking about, reading about, writing about and repeatedly watching *Ghost Light*, I still find it enjoyable. It still has aspects to reveal.

When working on a project like this, on a story with this level of complexity, every viewing reveals something new. Every night spent thinking about the story produces a new angle or relationship or parallel or reference. It's immensely rewarding but it's also immensely frustrating, as what this means is that the project is never truly finished. I just have to reach a point where I decide to stop. I can guarantee that long after this book is finished and printed and out there in the world for all to see, that I will be

---

[188] And of course the fat cheque and broad acclaim that will no doubt find me as a result.

kicking myself for things I didn't put in. Some of you will do the kicking for me, as I have either failed to notice or decided not to include the thoughts that *Ghost Light* evokes in you. That's the joy of *Ghost Light* in a world where so much art is disposable, digestible in a single sitting.

Those who express confusion over *Ghost Light* are right, and it's not because of the narrative density to which its difficulty is normally attributed. *Ghost Light* is a magic trick of a story. It uses the iconography of the haunted house story to tell a tale of aliens. It uses the language of evolution to talk about class. And just like any good magic trick, the audience's reaction is 'Do it again.'

BIBLIOGRAPHY

Books

1,001 Nights. Date unknown. Malcolm Lyons, trans, *Tales from 1,001 Nights: Aladdin, Ali Baba and Other Favourites*. London, Penguin, 2010. ISBN 9780141965871.

Arnold, Jon, *Rose*. **The Black Archive** #1. Edinburgh, Obverse Books, 2016. ISBN 9781909031401.

Austen, Jane, *Northanger Abbey*. London, John Murray, 1817.

Austen, Jane, and Ben H Winters, *Sense and Sensibility and Sea Monsters*. Philadelphia, Quirk Books, 2009. ISBN 978159474424.

Austen, Jane, and Seth Grahame-Smith, *Pride and Prejudice and Zombies*, Philadelphia, Quirk Books, 2009. ISBN 9781594743344.

The Bible, King James Version. 1611. Oxford, Oxford University Press, 1997. ISBN 9780192835253.

Bierce, Ambrose, *The Complete Short Stories of Ambrose Bierce*. Lincoln, Bison Books, 1984. ISBN 9780803260719.

Brock, Jason V, *Disorders of Magnitude: A Survey of Dark Fantasy*. Lanham, Rowman & Littlefield Publishers, 2014. ISBN 9781442235243.

Bucher-Jones, Simon, *Charles Dickens' Martian Notes*. Raleigh, Lulu.com, 2015. ISBN 9781326444518.

Bucher-Jones, Simon, *Image of the Fendahl*. **The Black Archive** #5. Edinburgh, Obverse Books, 2016. ISBN 9781909031418.

Burk, Graeme, *Who's 50: 50 Doctor Who Stories To Watch Before You Die – An Unofficial Companion*. Toronto, ECW Press, 2013. ISBN 9781770411661.

Conan Doyle, Arthur, *A Study in Scarlet*. London, Ward Lock & Co, 1887.

Conan Doyle, Arthur, *The Lost World*. London, Hodder & Stoughton, 1912.

Cooper, James Fenimore, *The Pioneers, or The Sources of the Susquehanna; a Descriptive Tale*. New York, Charles Wiley, 1823.

Cornell, Paul, Martin Day and Keith Topping, *Doctor Who: The Discontinuity Guide*. London, Virgin Publishing, 1995. ISBN 9780426204428.

Danielewski, Mark Z, *House of Leaves*. New York, Pantheon, Random House, 2000. ISBN 0375703764.

Darwin, Charles, *On the Origin of Species by Means of Natural Selection, or the Preservation of Favoured Races in the Struggle for Life*. London, John Murray, 1859.

Du Maurier, Daphne, *Rebecca*. London, Victor Gollancz, 1938.

Du Maurier, George, *Trilby*. Leipzig, Bernhard Tauchnitz, 1894.

The Epic of Gilgamesh. C2100 BCE. Maureen Gallery Kovacs, trans, Stanford, Stanford University Press, 1989. ISBN 9780804717113.

Farmer, Philip Jose, *Doc Savage: His Apocalyptic Life*. New York, Doubleday, 1973. ISBN 9780385084888.

Farmer, Philip Jose, *Tarzan Alive: A Definitive Biography of Lord Greystoke*. New York, Doubleday, 1972. ISBN 9780385038867.

Haggard, H Rider, *King Solomon's Mines.* London, Cassell and Co, 1885.

Hanson, Jay, *The Amityville Horror.* Upper Saddle River NJ, Prentice Hall, 1977.

Hawthorne, Nathaniel, *The House of the Seven Gables.* Boston, Ticknor and Fields, 1851.

Huxley, Julian, *Evolution: The Modern Synthesis.* Crows Nest, George Allen and Unwin, 1942.

James, Henry, *The Turn of the Screw.* London, William Heinemann, 1898.

King, Stephen, *The Shining.* New York, Doubleday, 1977. ISBN 9780385121675.

Miles, Lawrence, *Alien Bodies*, London, BBC Books, 1997. ISBN 9780563405771.

Nevins, Jess, *Heroes & Monsters: The Unofficial Companion to the League of Extraordinary Gentlemen.* Austin, MonkeyBrain Books, 2003. ISBN 9781932265040.

Parkin, Lance, *The Doctor Who Fanzine Archives.* **Time Unincorporated** #1. Des Moines, Mad Norwegian Press, 2009. ASIN B005CF78TE.

Pattie, Frank, *Mesmer and Animal Magnetism.* Hamilton, Edmonston Publishing, 1994. ISBN 9780962239359.

Platt, Marc, *Ghost Light.* **Doctor Who: The Scripts.** London, Titan Books Ltd, 1993. ISBN 9781852864774.

Platt, Marc, *Ghost Light*. **The Target Doctor Who Library** #149. London, Target Books, 1990. ISBN 9780426203513.

Platt, Marc, *Lungbarrow*. **Doctor Who: The New Adventures**. London, Virgin Publishing Ltd, 1997. ISBN 9780426205029.

Rand, Ayn, *Atlas Shrugged*. New York, Random House, 1957. OCLC 412355486.

Rohmer, Sax, *The Mystery of Dr Fu Manchu*. London, Methuen, 1913.

Ronson, Jon, *Lost at Sea*. London, Picador, 2012. ISBN 9781447222576.

Shelley, Mary, *Frankenstein: Or the Modern Prometheus*. London, Lackington, Hughes, Harding, Mavor and Jones, 1818.

Spencer, Herbert, *Principles of Biology*. London, Williams and Norgate, 1864.

Stevenson, Robert Louis, *Strange Case of Dr Jekyll and Mr Hyde*. London, Longmans, Green & Co, 1886.

Stoker, Bram, *Dracula*. London, Archibald Constable and Co, 1897.

Tutt, James William, *Melanism and Melanochronism in British Lepidoptera*. London, S Sonnenschein and Co, 1891.

Wells, HG, *The Invisible Man*. London, C Arthur Pearson, 1897.

Well, HG, *The Island of Dr Moreau*. London, Heinemann, Stone & Kimball, 1896.

Periodicals

Doctor Who Magazine (DWM). Marvel UK, Panini, BBC, 1979-.

Auger, David and Stephen James Walker, 'Sydney Newman Interview'. DWM #141, October 1988.

Owen, Dave, '27 Up'. DWM #255, August 1997.

Bishop, David, 'Andrew Cartmel Interview'. *TSV* #40. New Zealand Doctor Who Fan Club, July 1994.

Famous Monsters of Filmland #155. New York, Warren Publishing, July 1979.

Hodgson, Geoffrey M, 'Social Darwinism in Anglophone Academic Journals: A Contribution to the History of the Term', *Journal of Historical Sociology* vol 17 #4. Hoboken, John Wiley & Sons, December 2004.

Moore, Alan and Ian Gibson, **The Ballad of Halo Jones**. Serialised in *2000 AD*, London, Fleetway, 1984-86.

Moore, Alan, and Kevin O'Neill, **The League of Extraordinary Gentlemen**. ABC, Wildstorm, DC Comics, Top Shelf Comics, 1999-.

Poe, Edgar Allan, 'The Facts in the Case of M Valdemar'. *The American Review*, Wiley and Putnam, December 1845.

The Westminster Review. John Chapman, 1824-1914.

Spencer, Herbert, 'Progress: Its Law and Cause'. April 1857.

Spencer, Herbert, 'The Social Organism'. January 1860.

Television

American Horror Story: Murder House. Brad Falchuk Teley-Vision, Ryan Murphy Productions, 20th Century Fox Television, 2011.

Angel. Mutant Enemy Productions, Greenwolf Corp, Kuzui Enterprises, Sandollar Television, 20th Century Fox Television, 1999-2004.

Arrow. Berlanti Productions, DC Entertainment, Warner Bros Television, 2012-.

Buffy the Vampire Slayer. Mutant Enemy Productions, Kuzui Enterprises, Sandollar Television, 20th Century Fox Television, 1997-2003.

Doctor Who. BBC, 1963-.

Downton Abbey. Carnival Film & Television, Masterpiece Theatre, 2010-2015.

The Flash. Berlanti Productions, DC Entertainment, Warner Bros Television, 2014-.

Fargo. 26 Keys Productions, The Littlefield Co, Nomadic Pictures, Mike Zoss Productions, FX Productions, MGM Television, 2014-.

Hannibal. Dino de Laurentiis Co, Living Dead Guy Productions, AXN Original Productions, Gaumont International Television, 2013-2015.

Marvel's Agents of SHIELD. ABC Studios, Marvel Studios, Mutant Enemy, 2013-.

Marvel's Jessica Jones. ABC Studios, Marvel Studios, Netfix, Tall Girl Productions, 2015-.

Scooby Doo, Where Are You!. Hanna-Barbera Productions, 1969-71.

Smallville. Tollin, Robbins Productions, Millar Gough Ink, Warner Bros Television, DC Comics, Smallville Films, 2001-2011.

Supernatural. Kripke Enterprises, Warner Bros Television, Wonderland Sound and Vision, Supernatural Films, 2005-.

The Twilight Zone. Cayuga Productions, Inc, CBS Productions, 1959-64.

> *Five Characters in Search of an Exit*, 1961.

Film

Aldrich, Robert, dir, *Kiss Me Deadly*. Parklane Pictures Inc, 1955.

Asquith, Anthony, and Leslie Howard, dirs, *Pygmalion*. Gabriel Pascal Productions, 1938.

Bergman, Ingmar, dir, *The Seventh Seal*. Svensk Filmindustri, 1957.

Brooks, Mel, dir, *Young Frankenstein*. Gruskoff/Venture Films, Crossbow Productions, Jouer Ltd, 1974.

Cox, Alex, dir, *Repo Man*. Edge City, 1984.

Del Toro, Guillermo, dir. *Crimson Peak*. Legendary Pictures, 2015.

Fincher, David, dir, *Seven*. Cecchi Gori Pictures, Juno Pix, New Line Cinemas, 1995.

Fleming, Victor, dir, *Gone with the Wind*. Selznick International Pictures, MGM, 1939.

Guest, Val, dir, *The Quatermass Xperiment*. Hammer Films, 1955.

Hooper, Tober, dir, *Poltergeist*. MGM, Amblin Entertainment, SLM Production Group, 1982.

Jones, Charles M, dir, *Duck Dodgers in the 24½th Century*. Warner Bros, 1953.

Kenan, Gil, dir, *Poltergeist*. Fox 2000 Pictures, MGM, Ghost House Pictures, Vertigo Entertainment, TSG Entertainment, 2015.

Kubrick, Stanley, dir, *The Shining*. Warner Bros, Hawk Films, Peregrine, Producers Circle, 1980.

Natali, Vincenzo, dir, *Cube*. Feature Film Project, Odeon Films, Viacom Canada, Ontario Film Development Corp, Cube Libre, Telefilm Canada, Harold Greenberg Fund, 1997.

Nyby, Christian, dir, *The Thing from Another World*. RKO Radio Pictures, Winchester Pictures Corporation, 1951.

Sekely, Steve, dir, *The Day of the Triffids*. Allied Artists Pictures, Security Pictures Ltd, 1963.

Sharman, Jim, dir, *The Rocky Horror Picture Show*. 20th Century Fox Corp, Michael White Productions, 1975.

Tarantino, Quentin, dir, *Pulp Fiction*. Miramax, A Band Apart, Jersey Films, 1994.

Wan, James, dir, *The Conjuring*. New Line Cinema, Safran Company, Evergreen Media Group, 2013.

Watkins, James, dir, *The Woman in Black*. Cross Creek Pictures, Hammer Films, Alliance Films, UK Film Council, Talisman Productions, Exclusive Media Group, Film Vast, Filmgate Films, 2012.

Whale, James, dir, *Frankenstein*. Universal Pictures, 1931.

Stage Plays

Shaw, George Bernard, *Pygmalion*. 1913.

Lerner, Alan Jay and Frederick Loewe, *My Fair Lady*. 1956.

Music

Bonzo Dog Doo Dah Band, 'Hunting Tigers Out in Indiah'. Liberty Records, 1969.

Devo, 'Are We Not Men? We Are Devo!'. Warner Bros, 1978.

Queen and David Bowie, 'Under Pressure'. EMI/Elektra, 1981.

Vanilla Ice, 'Ice Ice Baby'. SBK Records, 1989.

Radio

The Green Hornet. Mutual Broadcasting System, 1936-52.

The Hitchhiker's Guide to the Galaxy. BBC Radio 4, 1978-79

The Lone Ranger. Mutual Broadcasting System, 1933-56.

Websites

'All Day Track Listing'. Illegal Tracklist. http://www.illegal-tracklist.net/Tracklists/AllDay. Accessed 5 March 2016.

'Doctor Who: The Classic Series: Ghost Light'. BBC online. http://www.bbc.co.uk/doctorwho/classic/episodeguide/ghostlight/detail.shtml. Accessed 5 March 2016.

Anders, Charlie Jane, 'Doctor Who's Steven Moffat: the io9 interview', *io9*, 18 May 2010.

http://io9.gizmodo.com/5542010/doctor-whos-steven-moffat-the-io9-interview. Accessed 5 March 2016.

Cutting, James E, et al, 'Quicker, faster, darker: Changes in Hollywood film over 75 years'. *i-Perception*, 30 September, 2011. http://www.ncbi.nlm.nih.gov/pmc/articles/PMC3485803/. Accessed 5 March 2016.

Harvati, Katerina, 'What Happened to the Neanderthals?'
Nature.com, 2012.
http://www.nature.com/scitable/knowledge/library/what-
happened-to-the-neanderthals-68245020. Accessed 5 March 2016.

McLean, Gareth, 'Steven Moffat: The Man with a Monster of a Job',
The Guardian, 22 March 2010.
http://www.guardian.co.uk/media/2010/mar/22/stephen-moffat-
doctor-who. Accessed 5 March 2016.

We Hunted the Mammoth.
http://www.wehuntedthemammoth.com. Accessed 5 March 2016.

BIOGRAPHY

Jonathan Dennis is the co-author (with Simon Bucher-Jones) of *The Brakespeare Voyage*. He has contributed to the **Faction Paradox**, **Iris Wildthyme**, **Señor 105**, and **Bernice Summerfield** ranges. He has also written for various websites and newspapers, and written and performed on radio. He lives in California with his wife and a cat that acts like a dog.